ENCHANTING FRIENDS

Collectible Poohs, Raggedies, Golliwoggs, and Roosevelt Bears with Price Guide

DEE HOCKENBERRY

Photography by Tom Hockenberry

Schiffer Publishing Ltd

77 Lower Valley Road, Atglen, PA 19310

Acknowledgments

In addition to the people and institutions mentioned in the preface, I would like to thank the following who either entrusted their treasures to be photographed or sent photographs to be included.

Judy Armitstead, Dottie Ayers, Candy Brainard, Alice Channing, Cynthia s Country Store, Doris Frohnsdorff, Susan Koenker, Phyllis Kransberg, Barbara Lauver, Susan Brown Nicholson, Sally Winey and Lori Woo.

I would also like to thank Nancy Schiffer for her faith and interest in this project. AND

Special Hugs to Maria Bluni, Bill Boyd and Larry Vaughan who came to my rescue when I really needed it.

This book makes reference to "Winnie The Pooh" and various other characters from A. A. Milne's book *Winnie The Pooh*. The copyright to all of the characters from the Disney version of *Winnie The Pooh* are owned by The Walt Disney Company.

The author has made every effort to find copyright holders. She apologizes for any omissions and these will be corrected in future editions upon notification to the publisher.

The copyrights for all A.A. Milne books are held by Methuen Children's Books Ltd. London and E.P. Dutton, N.Y. Reproduced by permission.

Sketches from the *Pooh Sketchbook* © 1982 Lloyds Bank Ltd. and Colin Anthony Richards executors of the estate of E.H. Shepard and the E.H. Shepard Trust reproduced by permission of Curtis Brown, London. These include the original drawings obtained from Christies and the Victoria and Albert Museum.

Library of Congress Cataloging-in-Publication Data
Hockenberry, Dee.
    Enchanting friends: collectible Poohs, raggedies, Golliwoggs, and Roosevelt bears with price guide / Dee Hockenberry.
        p.   cm.
    Includes bibliographical references and index.
    ISBN: 0-88740-723-4 (soft)
    NK4894.U6H63   1995
    688.7'221'075--dc20   95-3970
                                           CIP
Copyright © 1995
by Dee Hockenberry

Printed in Hong Kong
ISBN: 0-88740-723-4

We are interested in hearing from authors
with book ideas on related topics.

Published by Schiffer Publishing Ltd.
77 Lower Valley Road
Atglen, PA 19310
Please write for a free catalog.
This book may be purchased from the publisher.
Please include $2.95 postage.
Try your bookstore first.

Contents

Preface

A Journey Through Time

When one has a life-long fascination for literature and history and a background in art, the gathering of material that embraced all these elements became, for me, a labor of love.

The Central Children's Room at the Donnel Center, a branch of the New York City Library, now house the featured players in *Winnie The Pooh*. Eeyore, Piglet, Tigger, Kanga and Pooh reside in a glass case inside a room with a large viewing window. Roo is absent since he was left behind in an orchard about 60 years ago. Normally one must see the animals through the window, but my husband Tom and I were allowed inside to photograph them; a rare privilege for which we are most grateful.

The animals lived with Christopher Milne, in Surrey, until 1947 when they left for an extended (10 year!) trip around the United States. In 1956 they were put on permanent display at the offices of the American publisher E.P. Dutton. They remained there until 11:00 A M Friday, September 11, 1987 when they were presented to the library. Justin Schiller, historian, described the toys as "the most important objects in 20th century children's literature." They have never been repaired, or even cleaned, for Mr. Milne preferred they be left as if a child had just finished playing with them. Their home insures that generations of children will forever be able to feast their eyes on familiar friends.

The Victoria And Albert Museum, in the South Kensington area of London, is not only a magnificent edifice, but is the proud owner of original E.H. Shepard drawings. Tom and I sat in the print room and reveled as portfolio after portfolio was placed before us. The 271 drawings contained both finished and preliminary sketches, all wonderful and an emotional experience to behold.

There really is a "100 Aker" woods, formally known as Ashdown Forest, in west Sussex. A long, long footpath leads from the car park to Pooh Sticks bridge and that, too, is a delightful treat for children young not only in years, but in heart.

The Swan Library, in my hometown, was helpful as always in my biographical search for data on Johnny Gruelle and his works. It was also, for me, a wonderful first experience to climb the steps between the imposing lions at the main branch of the New York City Library. It was here that I discovered Edith Lyttleton's biography of Florence Upton.

Ms. Edwina Ehrman assistant curator of the Department of Later London History, at the Museum of London, graciously opened her department for us on a day when visitors are not usually allowed to examine the archives. The original drawings of Florence Upton's book *The Golliwoggs Fox Hunt* was part of our pleasure, along with a letter from the donor's solicitors when they were presented.

Theodore Roosevelt plays a recurring role and intertwines with many aspects in this book. It is partially why we spent time exploring his past domains and absorbing his aura. Mr. Roosevelt's birthplace in New york City, his home at Oyster Bay, Long Island and his inauguration site in Buffalo, New York were among our quests. One must remember that without his role in the captured bear saga there would be no teddy bear, thus no Winnie The Pooh or Teddy B and Teddy G either. Our beloved president was also the butt of political cartoonists as are most public figures. John Gruelle's professional life included this occupation and, as a satirical artist for the Cleveland Press, included T.R. in his cartoons. One of T. R.'s children's favorite books was *The Wind In The Willows*, illustrated in a 1931 edition by Ernest Howard Shepard. Another link regardless of how tenuous. Life appears to be connected by threads that go on and on. I have included in the Roosevelt Bear/Eaton section a selection of objects portraying this man and his association with the bruin even though *they* are not fundamentally Eaton's creations. A book about any ursines would be lacking indeed if our 26th president's role were not included--if only in a small way.

Introduction

The Men, The Women, and Their "Music".

Talent. Genius. Both are innate traits that can lie dormant until an unexpected inspiration or a catalyst brings these qualities to the surface. Writers find, for the most part, that from an early age they possess a facility for the written word and from then on it is a matter of honing their craft. Still, until a certain spark electrifies their work they can remain unpublished. What a wondrous quality it is to be able to set down on paper poetry that speaks to one or prose as beautiful as poetry. It has been said that artists are born with a brush in their hand, for talent is usually evident in very young children. How admirable it is to be able to capture the essentials with just a few dextrous strokes.

A.A. Milne was already an established writer when he penned a *Gallery Of Children* in 1925. The characters, while pretty, lacked spirit and for this reason Milne looked further and found it in his son's nursery. Christopher Robin's teddy bear had made an appearance in *When We Were Very Young*, but it was with the publication of *Winnie The Pooh* that Milne became immortalized.

Winnie and his friends

Winnie-the-Pooh and Friends poster available at the Donnel Center, New York Public Library.

Since it is not unusual for one person to be multi-talented, it is not surprising that Johnny Gruelle both wrote and illustrated his work. His fairies and puckish creatures were drawn with unerring charm in both books and newspapers long before cruel fate had a hand in his destiny. When his young daughter, Marcella, died of a lingering illness, Johnny's monument to her was the Raggedy Ann stories, followed by Ann's image as the most enduring rag doll in America's history.

Florence K. Upton's lively imagination and a gift for drawing was encouraged by her mother, Bertha. In fact it was the mother who first suggested a collaboration with herself doing the writing and her daughter illustrating children's books. Florence found her inspiration when she came upon an old tattered blackamoor rag doll that was a remnant of her childhood and thus the Golliwogg was born----A hundred years legacy of delight.

When our president Theodore Roosevelt refused to shoot a captured bear cub, the incident was popularized in a cartoon. A jointed bear toy was introduced in both America and Germany at approximately the same time and the "Teddy Bear" came into being. Seymour Eaton, a writer at the time, was inspired by these events and wrote several tales calling the two bears Teddy B and Teddy G. Eventually the stories were assembled in book form and was closely followed by three others. *The Adventures Of The Roosevelt Bears* in turn inspired a myriad of companies to produce their image and are as collectible today as they were over 80 years ago.

The original Winnie-the-Pooh, photo taken through the glass case at the Children's Room of the New York Public Library.

Tigger and Winnie-the-Pooh on display at the New York Public Library.

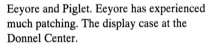

Eeyore and Piglet. Eeyore has experienced much patching. The display case at the Donnel Center.

Opposite Page Bottom Right Photo:
Original sketch by E.H. Shepard. Preliminary pencil drawings the artist made when first encountering the animals in 1924. Note that Pooh is drawn as he actually appeared before Shepard changed him to resemble his own son's teddy. *Courtesy of The Victoria and Albert Museum, London.*

Opposite Page Bottom Left Photo:
Original sketch by E.H. Shepard. Pooh and Mr. Sanders House. *Courtesy of the Victoria and Albert Museum, London*

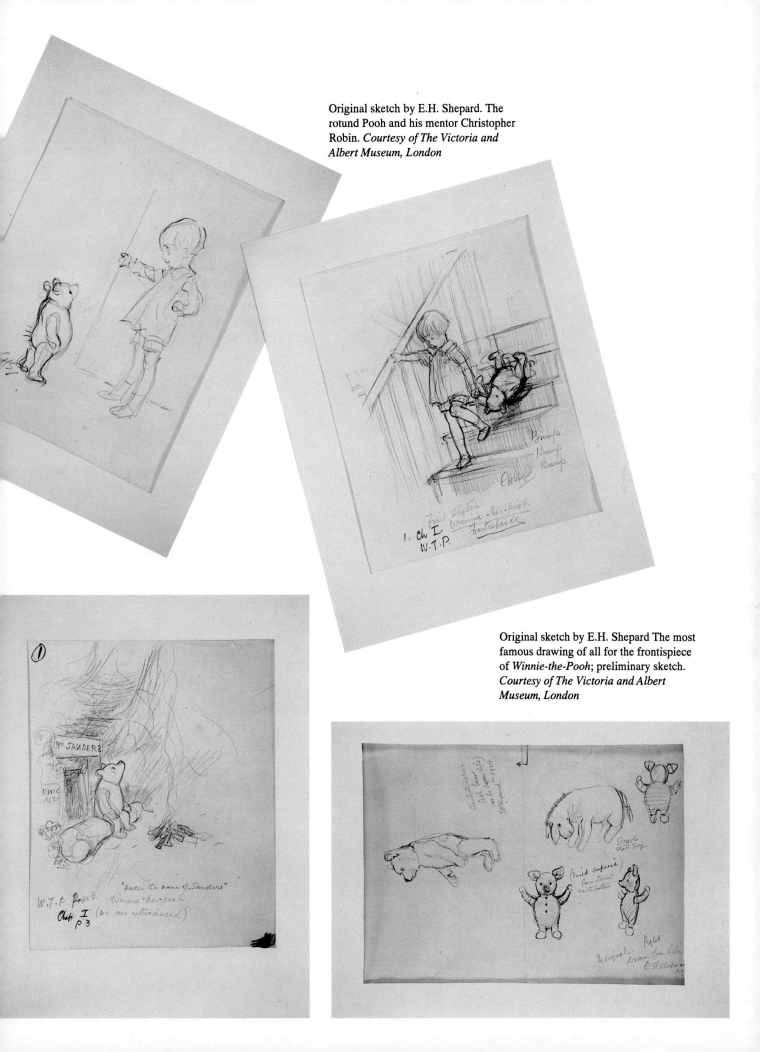

Original sketch by E.H. Shepard. The rotund Pooh and his mentor Christopher Robin. *Courtesy of The Victoria and Albert Museum, London*

Original sketch by E.H. Shepard The most famous drawing of all for the frontispiece of *Winnie-the-Pooh*; preliminary sketch. *Courtesy of The Victoria and Albert Museum, London*

Entering Ashdown Forest

View of Pooh-Sticks Bridge

Pooh Corner Gift Shop. A charming shop housed in a 300 year old Queen Anne building. It is located in Hartfield, Sussex, where long ago Christopher Robin, accompanied by his Nanny, shopped for the sweets known as Bull's-eyes.

Letter to Sir Guy Laking from Miss Moore's solicitors advising of her gift to the Museum of London. *Courtesy of the Museum of London.*

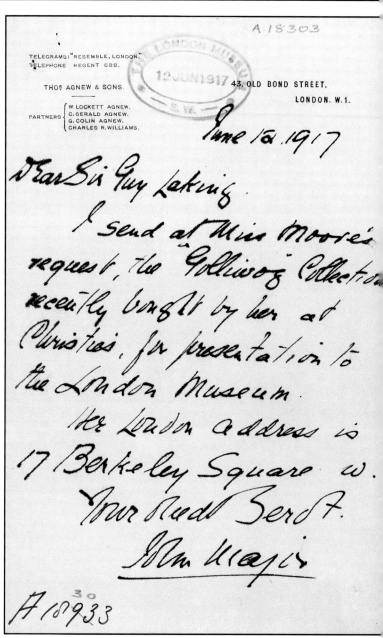

Teddy Roosevelt's birth site in New York City

The Trophy Room at Sagamore Hill

Front view of Sagamore Hill

The Bear rug at Oyster Bay

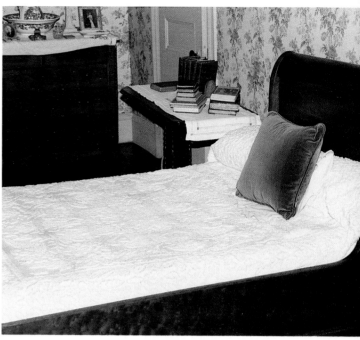

The bed where Theodore Roosevelt died
peacefully in his sleep, at Sagamore Hill.

Teddy Roosevelt's inaugural site in
Buffalo, N.Y.

Chapter One
Winnie the Pooh

The Beginning

When one envisions Winnie The Pooh the areas of London and south to Sussex comes to mind. Actually we can trace how it all began to Birmingham in the19th century, across the sea to Canada,and back to England. A circuitous route indeed, and one filled with drama and pathos. Harry Coleburn was born April 12, 1887 in the industrial city of Birmingham in Worcestershire. At the age of 18 he emigrated to Toronto Canada, became schooled in Veterinary medicine, and eventually relocated in Winnipeg,Manitoba to live and start his practice. When World War I broke out he joined the Army as a Captain in the Horse Infantry. On the way back to his homeland he stopped to rest at White River,Ontario and thus begins the tale of the first Winnie. The momentous day occurred in August of 1911 when the train pulled into the station of this small community. A trapper,with a small black bear cub,was the first thing the Captain spied upon alighting. Of course his compassionate heart cried out at the sight of this orphan whose mother had been slain for her skin. He adopted the baby as his company's mascot, for a price of $20, and named it "Winnipeg" in honor of his residence.

The little creature, nicknamed Winnie, traveled across the ocean arriving on the Salisbury Plains where the regiment began to train. When the troop was called into battle the dilemma of Winnie's care became imminent. After much deliberation and agonizing the London Zoo was decided upon and so,with much sadness,the Captain bade farewell to his special charge.

Bronze statue of Winnie at the gateway of the London Zoo

Bronze placque *Bear Cub* by Lorne McKean commemorating Winnie / friendly and famous / American Black Bear / mascot of Princess Pats / Canadian Regiment / who came to the Zoo / in 1914 while her / regiment went on / to fight in France / and who lived here / known and loved / by many children / until her death in 1934 / She gave her name to / WINNIE-THE-POOH / and / A.A. Milne and / Ernest Shepard gave / Winnie-the-Pooh to the world

Winnie was so accustomed to people by this time and had such a gentle nature that she allowed children to ride on her back. Her fame soon spread and she became the primary attraction at the zoo by children of all ages. One such child was a solemn faced boy named Christopher Robin who often visited what was to become his favorite animal.

When the war came to an end Captain Coleburn went back to the zoo to fetch the bear, but finding her so well cared for and content he was loathe to interrupt her life anew. With unselfish sadness he left her where she was, but stayed in England to further his education at a veterinary college. When the course was completed, after a year's time, he visited Winnie once more and then returned to his home in Canada.

Winnie and his saviour are commemorated in several places assuring their lives and times will live on. At the Gateway to the London Zoo a bronze statue and placque of the bear is dedicated to her memory. The Asseniboine Zoo in Winnipeg features a bronze statue of both man and ursine, but it is in White River, sight of their meeting, that the pair is honored in a spectacular way. Along with a wooden carved effigy of the pair, there is a museum and a yearly celebration. This August event attracts visitors by the score not only to pay homage to the Captain and the real bear, but to a boy and his faithful companion Winnie The Pooh.

Alan Alexander Milne and *Winnie The Pooh*

On January 18, 1882 the third and youngest son of the headmaster of HenleyHouse School, first saw the light of day. The child was named Alan Alexander Milne and was brought up in this scholastic environment on Mortimer Road in the London suburb of Hampstead. His innate intelligence was further developed by his surrounding and he began reading at the tender age of 2 1/2 years. Alan was precocious and imaginative declaring, at age seven, that he couldn't determine whether algebra was better than football or Euclid more delightful than sponge cake!

A photograph of him, taken when he was about four years old, pictures him with long, golden curls and dressed in a velvet suit with a lace collar. One can only ponder whether his mother longed for a girl or whether the outfit reflected on the novel *Little Lord Fauntleroy*, a book that was the current rage.

Throughout his life Alan was surrounded by the literati, beginning with H.G. Wells, who taught at the Henley School, and continuing on to college where he rubbed shoulders with Leonard Woolf, husband of Virginia. In 1893, when only eleven, he won a scholarship to Westminster Prep and in 1900 entered Trinity College at Cambridge. At this prestigious school Leonard Woolf, secretary of the Shakespeare Society, was instrumental in Milne's election as a member, during the spring of his second year.

Since Alan shared a facility for verse with his brother Ken, his first published works, appearing in *Granta*, the Cambridge magazine, used the by-line A.K. Milne; a utilization of both of their initials. By 1902 Alan was editing the publication, an early indication of his rapid rise in the world of letters.

When his formal education was completed, a small inheritance enabled him to live in London and pursue his life's work. He began writing on a free lance basis and made his first sale to *Vanity Fair* for the "princely" sum of 15 shillings. Alan then began selling both verse and prose to *Punch* the one-time anti-establishment periodical. In 1905 his first book *Lovers In London*, a collection of sketches was published and on February 13th of the following year he became assistant editor at *Punch*. An association with this satirical magazine seemed natural since being funny came to him with the same ease as breathing. He did,however,have his detractors and in later years came to detest the word "whimsical." A young artist by the name of Ernest Shepard, worked at Punch as well, but Milne dismissed him as hopeless and wondered what the art editor saw in him.

Alan's career continued on a successful curve, but he was into his fourth decade before settling down as a family man. On June 4, 1913 his marriage to Dorothy de Selincourt took place and she is the "Daphne" (a name she preferred,) that some of his books are dedicated to.

Although A.A. Milne was not considered an intellectual by the intelligentsia, he had a passion for using his brain and an abhorrence for violence, traits that effected everything he penned. In spite of his horror for war, his patriotism over rode his feelings and he joined the army during World War I. This cerebral man surprised even himself by becoming an expert at laying telephone lines and on signalling lamps, power buzzers, heliographs, morse code and semaphore.

Upon demobilization, he and Daphne took up residence at 11 Mallord Street in the London section of Chelsea, just a few minutes from Kings Road. It was at this house where, on August 21, 1920 a son, and their only child was born. The boy, christened Christopher Robin, referred to himself as Billy Moon- "Moon" being his pronunciation of his surname.

For Christopher's first birthday he was gifted with a teddy bear, bought at Harrods department store; a toy that became an absolute favorite and inseparable companion. The teddy was called by several different names in the beginning, but eventually the one that stuck was Winnie The Pooh. The original "Winnie" was the American black bear residing at the London Zoo, an animal so tame and loved that children could ride on his back. He was the main attraction and this included Christopher Robin who often visited him. "Pooh" came from the name of a swan who lived in Arundel Sussex, a town where the Milne family vacationed. Upon departure, they borrowed the name, thinking the swan wouldn't need it any more. Another soft toy, a donkey named Eeyore, joined the household as a Christmas present in 1921.

A. A. Milne and Christopher Robin, the most widely publicized photograph of father and son taken in 1926 by Howard Coster; it hangs in the National Portrait Gallery, London.

The Pooh books, are so enmeshed in Milne's name, that one tends to forget that he was also an established playwright, who not only dramatized Kenneth Grahame's *The Wind In The Willows*, but in 1922 had five plays running simultaneously. Three were in the United States, one was in London and another in Liverpool; surely a heady sensation.

During the summer of their son's fourth year, the family found what they had long desired--a weekend summer retreat. The house called Cotchford Farm, was in Sussex bordering on Ashdown Forest. A sixteen century cottage, with parts of it even older, it was in need of repair so a full year passed before residence was established. The house and surrounding woods would ultimately become the

The charming house on Mallord Street in London where A. A. Milne lived and Christopher Robin was born.

site, and figure so prominently, in the Pooh saga. It all started in an old walnut tree whose hollowed insides made the perfect abode for a five year old lad and his Teddy. Trees always played a prominent role in the books since that was how it was in real life.

While A.A. Milne and his son were experiencing the joys of life with Pooh, an old associate was on the horizon. Ernest H. Shepard, the man responsible for forming our mental image of Pooh, would soon become an integral part of the Milne's world. Shepard, also a complex individual, always resented his lack of formal education having been encouraged all his life to put his energies into drawing and painting. Since this led to his winning a scholarship to art school, we must disagree with Milne's first assessment of his talent. It is interesting to note, as well, that Shepard's son also had a bear (around 1915) that was a household member. "Growler's" doings were told in a letter written by his father to the boy, Graham, when he was seven. It is obvious, and safe to assume, that this family had a special association with a bear, too, and probably accounts for Shepard's whole hearted response to the project. When the actual drawings of Pooh were formalized, Ernest, who preferred working from a model, used Growler as the subject.

In March of 1926 Shepard visited the Milne's house to meet the toys and it was decided to make Piglet smaller because of references in the book. At this time he drew an almost exact replica of Christopher Robin's appearance right down to the window-pane checked smock, short trousers and distinctive haircut. The child was dressed in his mother's ideas but the smocks were sewn by Nanny who also cut his hair.

At this juncture, Milne reversed his opinion of Shepard's artistry and was thoroughly delighted with the very first sketch. *When We Were Very Young* was published in London on November 6, 1924 and in New York on November 20th, with a dedication to Billy Moon. Shepard had accepted a lump sum of £50 for the illustrations, but the day after publication received a £100 bonus. Subsequently, in a warm and generous gesture, Milne suggested that Shepard have a permanent share in the royalties, thereby recognizing his very important contribution. The first printing was an issue of 5,140, plus a special edition of 110 on handmade paper. Less than eight weeks later the sales and reprintings totaled 43,843 and the tome was established as the greatest children's book since *Alice In Wonderland*. Even Kermit and Theodore Roosevelt Junior were so entranced that they called upon the Milne's London house to have their copies autographed.

The rights to reproduce the drawings as toys, wallpaper and various other related items was granted in both England and the United States in the mid 1920s. Eeyore, Piglet and Pooh were already ensconced in the nursery, but it was determined that if future books were to be written, additional characters would be needed. So, on a deliberate trip to the toy department at Harrods, a choice of Kanga and Roo was decided upon. Owl and Rabbit were the inventions of the authors creative mind.

As early as 1925, Carl Pforzheimer, an extremely rich book collector, began to collect manuscripts and typescripts. He purchased some original material from both Milne and Shepard and when he died his Pooh collection was sold by Sothebys in 1986 for £120,000. However, shortly after Alan had sold his items to Carl he regretted it and kept his Winnie The Pooh works, eventually leaving them in his will to the Wren Library at Trinity College, Cambridge.

The second book, *Winnie The Pooh*, came out October 14, 1926 in London and two weeks later in New York. The first printing was for 32,000, but sold 150,000 before the year ended. The sly wit appealed even more to adults than to the children it was intended for. In 1927, *Now We Are Six* appeared with a dedication to Christopher Robin from his father. "For my Moon From his Blue Now I Am 45" By this time the publisher increased the first edition to 50,000 and by the time *The House At Pooh Corners* came out in 1928, the first printing was for 75,000. Within a very short time-span the world wide distribution of all four volumes could be counted in the millions, and by the 1930s Pooh was an industry.

In January of 1929, just three months after the final book was published, Christopher Robin started Prep School at Gibbs on Sloane Square in London. Clearly it was time to leave the forest and he told his faithful friend Pooh, that he wasn't going anymore. Although Pooh wept when he realized that there would be no more books, he was reassured that his place in literature was indeed safe. It seemed best, from the father's perspective to stop while the books were still popular and to shield his son from further publicity.

In the ending of *The House At Pooh Corners* a small lad and a rotund bear go off together to the top of the forest. We, who have known and adored this remarkable duo can always remember them at play. And then..it isnt really goodbye for we are reassured that the forest will always be there and that anyone friendly with bears can always find it.

The Universal Pooh And Company

Although Winnie The Pooh is only mentioned briefly in *When We Were Very Young*, it is still considered the first volume in the following quartet of collectible issues. By virtue of being the smallest first edition printing, it is also the hardest to locate.

1. *When We Were Very Young* © 1924
2. *Winnie The Pooh* © 1926
3. *Now We Are Six* © 1927
4. *The House At Pooh Corners* © 1928

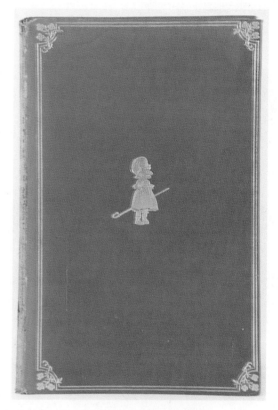

When We Were Very Young special edition bound in leather with gold tooled decorations on front and on spine; gold leaf end papers; produced in this special way to celebrate the 10th printing in July 1925; Methuen, London.

The American publishers, E.P. Dutton & Co., were preceded in publication by the London firm of Methuen by about one month. Each hardbound edition measures 5 inches by 7 1/2 inches and originally had protective dust jackets. Some of the special copies were leather bound with lettering and Shepard designs blocked in gilt.

Since first editions command high prices, it is not unusual to see special copies sky rocket, such as a volume signed by both Milne and Shepard fetching over $8,000. The record, thus far, has been £16,500, sold at Christie's Auction House, for Shepard's own copy of an American edition inscribed for him by Milne. In the summer of 1993 an English bookseller offered, for sale, a set of all four books, mint with dust jackets and autographed by the author for £4,500 (or about $6,800 at the time.) It is not only the books but the illustrations that are highly coveted. The first drawing in *Winnie The Pooh*, and probably the most universally recognized, is that of Christopher Robin pulling Pooh downstairs. It sold in December of 1991 for £18,700, a tidy sum indeed. Occasionally other drawings surface, are offered at auction, and create quite a stir, followed by excited bidding.

Other early books are *The Christopher Robin Story Book* © 1929 and *Verses* © 1932. These books are versions of the first ones, but with the addition of some new illustrations. Given the great popularity of the poems in *When We Were Very Young*, most of them were set to music and appeared in print in the form of song books.

1. *Fourteen Songs* © 1924
2. *The King's Breakfast* © 1925
3. *Teddy Bear And Other Songs* © 1926
4. *Songs From Now We Are Six* © 1927
5. *More Very Young Songs* © 1928
6. *The Hums of Pooh* © 1929

The immense admiration of all the books is enormous in scope, with the English editions alone, still selling a half a million copies annually.

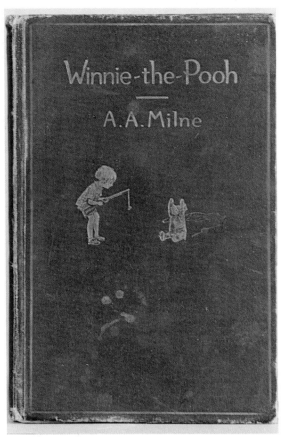

The book *Winnie-the-Pooh* by A.A. Milne; 1926; E.P. Dutton and Company; first edition; Ernest H. Shepard illustrations.

Of course it didn't end with just the quartet, spin offs, and song books. Related books and objects began immediately and continue to the present. Cooking, pop-ups, sticker, and work-out are but a few of the books that are published yearly by both Methuen and Dutton. Of great interest are the early versions of the "Pooh" and "Very Young" calendars and the *Christopher Robin Birthday Book*. Various magazines and newspapers continually printed new and interesting material and while not easy to find, the search is worth the effort.

Perhaps the most remarkahle work to result from the world's love at the rotund bear is that written by a Hungarian doctor. *Winnie-Ille-Pu*, a Latin translation by Alexander Lenard, was published in 1960 and has the honor of being the first book written in Latin to be on the New York Times best seller list. Dr. Lenard was born in Budapest in 1910, educated at the Therasinum in Vienna, and eventually emmigrated to Brazil. He was fluent in twelve languages and first translated Pooh in German, a feat that earned him a personal congratulation from Milne himself. In 1965 he told of how he came to write the Latin version in his book *The Valley Of The Latin Bear*. It took him seven years, refining the draft several times, and by re-reading the classics to find poetic solutions. By the 1980 revision of the E.P. Dutton publication it had seen 21 printings.

Besides the Latin, people from all countries have the opportunity to read the books in their own language. Translations include Afrikaans, Breton, Bulgarian, Castilian, Catalan, Chinese, Czek, Danish, Dutch, Esperanto, Finnish, French, German, Greek, Hungarian, Icelandic, Italian, Japanese, Macedonian, Norwegian, Polish, Portugese, Romanian, Serbo-Croat, Slovak, Slovene, Swedish and Thai.

Since the Walt Disney Company obtained the license in the 1960s, many books, most notably the "Golden Books," have featured Pooh in their cartoon version, along with many other items under the Disney copyright.

I doubt if there is a child in the world who has not been enraptured by Pooh. In Warsaw there is a street called "Ulica Kubusia Puchatka" with an engraving on the sign of Pooh and Piglet. I suspect as well, that visitors to any country might very well stumble upon our illustrious friend in seemingly unlikely spots. We can stare in amazement, smile, and murmur "Hello old friend."

Now We Are Six back cover, gold tooled graphic of Pooh and Piglet on bottom right.

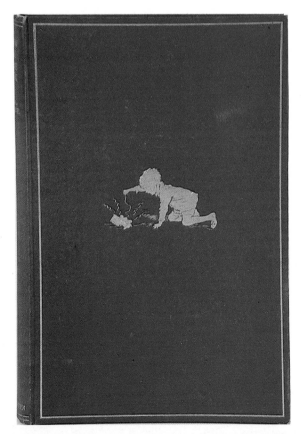

Now We Are Six, first edition by Methuen, gold tooled graphic on cover and title on spine, 1927

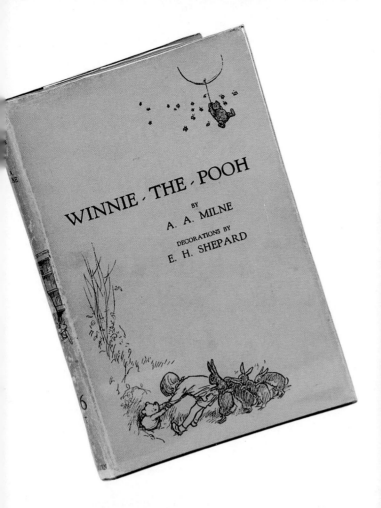

Winnie the Pooh, 5th edition, 1927
showing original dust jacket; published by
Methuen, London.

THE

ORIGINAL DRAWINGS

BY

ERNEST H. SHEPARD

ILLUSTRATING

"NOW WE ARE SIX"

WILL BE EXHIBITED DURING

DECEMBER, 1927

AT

The Sporting Gallery

32 King Street, Covent Garden

LONDON

Advertisement sheet announcing the
showing of Ernest H. Shepard's original
drawings; found in first edition copies of
Now We Are Six published by Methuen.

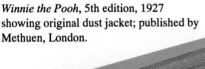

Now We Are Six, A. A. Milne, first edition,
E. P. Dutton & Co, 1927

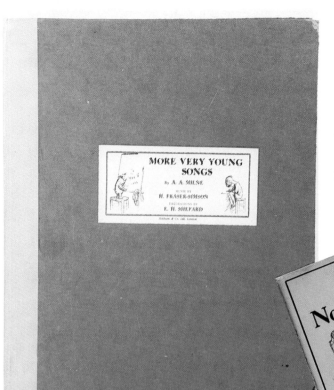

Song book *More Very Young Songs*, larger format of 10 inches X 12 inches; 1st edition 1928; Methuen, London; words by A.A.Milne; music by H. Fraser-Simson; drawings by E.H. Shepard; contains "Us Two," "Knights and Ladies," "In the Dark," "Shoes and Stockings," "Forgiven," "Binker," "Nursery Chairs," "Waiting at the Window," "Spring Morning," and "The End."

More Very Young Songs complete with dust jacket, published by Methuen in 1928. *Songs From Now We Are Six* complete with dust jacket, published by Methuen in 1927. Both books have verses by Milne, music by H. Fraser-Simson and illustrations by Shepard.

The House at Pooh Corner first edition with dust jacket published by Methuen & Co. Ltd., 36 Essex Street, London W.C., 1928; the English version precedes the American publication by about a month; the last book in which we say goodbye to Christopher Robin and his friends.

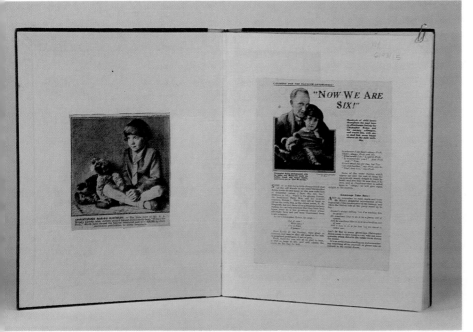

Newspaper clippings of the period. Interesting photos of Christopher Robin, Winnie the Pooh and A.A. Milne found pasted inside the cover of *Songs From Now We Are Six;* printed material from the 1920s is not easy to come by and, for this writer, adds immeasurably to the value of the book. © *Methuen*

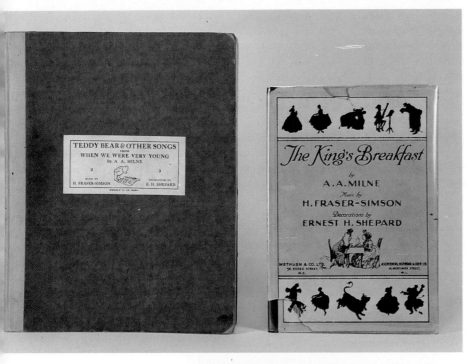

Teddy Bear & Other Songs. Verses by A. A. Milne from the book *When We Were Very Young;* music by H. Fraser-Simson, published by Methuen in 1926; dedication inside reads "By permission of Her Royal Highness The Dutchess of York these songs are dedicated to The Princess Elizabeth" (Queen Elizabeth II). *The King's Breakfast* complete with dust jacket; verse by Milne, music by H. Fraser-Simpson, published by Methuen in 1925.

Pooh cotton fabric; 72 in X 54 in; Christopher Robin, Pooh and all the animals are featured; Shepard renditions; England; circa 1935.

Winnie the Pooh and the Bees pop-up book published by Methuen in the 1950s; colorful and desirable with four pop-ups, one of which is shown.

The World of Pooh, E.P. Dutton, 1957, new issue containing *Winnie the Pooh* and *The House at Pooh Corner*, new illustrations, some in full color.

Winnie the Pooh, A.A. Milne, illustrated by Mary and Wallace Stover, Perks Publishing, 1944, soft cover.

Winnie-the-Pooh The Honey Tree, a Little
Golden Book, Walt Disney, 10th printing,
1974.

The Pooh Cook Book, published by
Methuen, 1971, recipes by Katie Stewart,
illustrated by Ernest H. Shepard.

The Enchanted Places by Christopher
Milne, first American edition, 1957, E.P.
Dutton. *Lori Woo Collection*

Magazine pages with a new story
by A.A. Milne and Shepard
drawings; *Ladies Home Journal*;
December 1927.

Pooh's Pot O'Honey, small format 2 1/2
in. (6 cm) X 3 3/4 in. (10 cm), four books
in presentation box, E. P. Dutton Inc.,
1968.

The Path Through the Trees, first
American edition, 1979, Christopher
Milne, E. P. Dutton. *Lori Woo Collection*

Children's Digest magazine published by
Parent's Magazine in 1970, a 6-page story
of Pooh and Piglet hunting with black and
white illustrations. *Pu der Bär*, another
version of the German translation by
Dressler, issue of 1990.

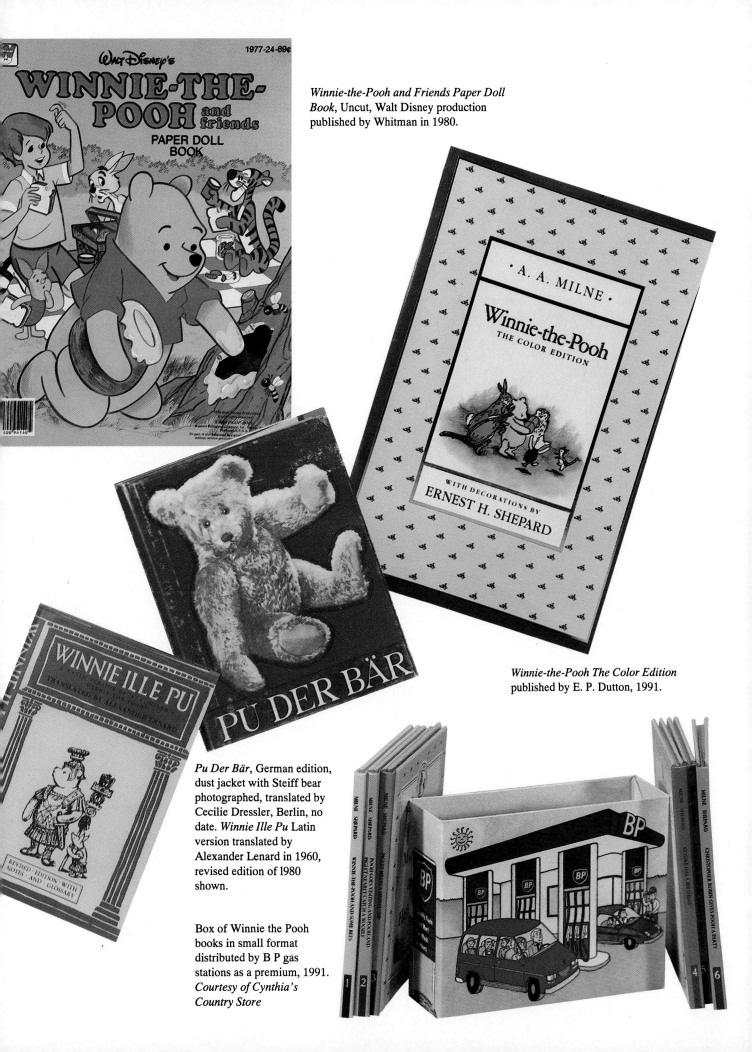

Winnie-the-Pooh and Friends Paper Doll Book, Uncut, Walt Disney production published by Whitman in 1980.

Winnie-the-Pooh The Color Edition published by E. P. Dutton, 1991.

Pu Der Bär, German edition, dust jacket with Steiff bear photographed, translated by Cecilie Dressler, Berlin, no date. *Winnie Ille Pu* Latin version translated by Alexander Lenard in 1960, revised edition of 1980 shown.

Box of Winnie the Pooh books in small format distributed by B P gas stations as a premium, 1991. *Courtesy of Cynthia's Country Store*

"Handsome bell rope isn't it," said owl. An original drawing by Ernest H. Shepard, 10 1/2 in. (26 cm) x 8 in. (20 cm), signed with initials and inscribed by the artist; rendered in pencil, pen, and black ink; similar to an illustration in *Winnie the Pooh* © 1926, which sold at Christies auction house in London on July 18, 1990 for £18,700. *Courtesy of Christies, South Kensington*

"Tigger comes to the forest," original drawing by Ernest H. Shepard, 12 1/2 in. (32 cm) x 10 in. (25 cm) rendered in pencil, pen, and black ink; signed and inscribed by artist; similar to illustration in *The House at Pooh Corner*.© 1928; sold July 18, 1990 for £18,700 at Christies auction house in London. *Courtesy of Christies, South Kensington*

"Tiggers can't climb trees," original drawing by Ernest H. Shepard 14 1/2 in. (37 cm) x lO 1/2 in. (26 cm) rendered in pencil, pen and black ink; signed and inscribed by artist; similar to illustration in *The House at Pooh Corner*, © 1928, sold July 18, 1990 for £20,000 at Christies Auction House, London. *Courtesy of Christies, South Kensington*

Huggable Poohs

Even though the "real" Winnie The Pooh bears little resemblance to the Shepard rendition, we still hold Farnell, the maker, in high esteem. Clearly that wondrous teddy possessed a charm that brought out the imaginations of both A.A. Milne and his young son.

Soon after the book's release many firms on both sides of the Atlantic began producing the characters. Among the English makers were the Teddy Co., Chad Valley, John Addams, Ann Wilkinson and Gabrielle Designs (who currently hold the license under Disney.) Joy Toys, a company in Australia, began designing their version in 1967.

In the United States, Stephen Slesinger Inc. obtained the copyright and, over the years, had several companies or artists designing their versions. The first appears to have been F.W. Woolnough Co. in 1930. During the late 1940s, and into the following decade, Agnes Brush made her impact by crafting the whole team with wit and ingenuity. The last to work under the Slesinger label was Knickerbocker, an established company, still producing other quality teddies.

In 1964, when Disney obtained the rights, Gund made small velvet animals, but over the years evolved into the use of plush. Along with Cal Toys, of California they manufactured the Pooh items sold in the Sears stores. Gund is also the supplier of the toys sold through the Disney outlets, including those within the parks.

Perhaps the most faithful to Shepard's creations, and our mental image are those designed by American artist R. John Wright. Beginning in 1985, his doll Christopher Robin, along with Pooh, took the market by storm and continues to do so.

Chronologically, his magic examples are:

1. Christopher Robin And Pooh 1985, 1986
2. 8 in. Pooh 1985, 1986
3. 5 1/2 in. Piglet 1985, 1986
4. Eeyore 1986, 1987
5. Kanga & Roo 1986, 1987
6. Tigger 1986, 1987
7. Christopher Robin II 1986, 1987
8. 9 in. Piglet 1986, 1987
9. 18 in. Pooh 1986, 1987
10. Pooh with Honeypot 1988, 1989
11. 7 1/2 in. Piglet with violets 1988, 1989
12. Pooh with chair 1988, 1989
13. 5 in. Pocket Pooh 1993
14. 2 1/2 in. Pocket Piglet 1994

Kanga, 12 in. (31 cm) and Roo, 5 1/2 in. (14 cm) made by Agnes Brush with permission of Stephen Slesinger Inc., 1950s. Kanga is rust and tan felt with an embroidered circle for nose and bead eyes; Roo is rust and brown felt with embroidered eyes. *Alice Channing Collection*

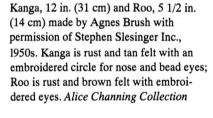

Winnie the Pooh, 13 in. (33 cm) made by Agnes Brush, Whitestone, L.I., with permission of Stephen Slesinger Inc., 1950s, tan flannel with black nose as part of pattern, shoe button eyes, red jersey vest. *Alice Channing Collection*

Carol Stewart, known for delightful minatures, has presented her interpretations at some of the Disney World Conventions held each year in Florida.

Pooh is such a lovable bear and evokes such nostalgic memories of our childhood, or our children's, that his image is collected with not only zeal, but great affection.

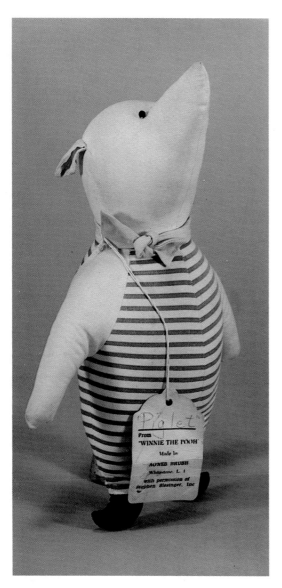

Piglet, 11 in. (28 cm) made by Agnes Brush with permission of Stephen Slesinger Inc., 1950S, off-white cotton with green striped suit and black feet part of the pattern; pink removeable tie, black bead eyes, original tag that leaves room for animal's name. *Alice Channing Collection*

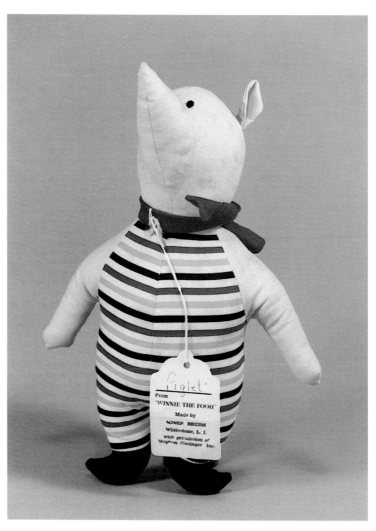

Piglet, 11 in. (28 cm) Another version of clothing worn by Agnes Brush's Piglet, retains original paper hang tag. *Barbara Lauver Collection*

Piglet hang tag of heavy weight paper with cotton cord; used for all animals made by Agnes Brush; they were all printed alike and the animals name was added in hand printing. Although each toy originally came with one, today it is hard to find an animal with it still attached.

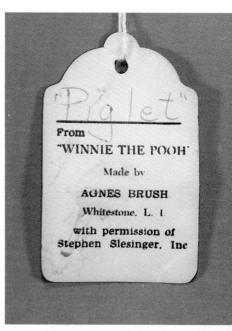

Tigger, 14 in. by Agnes Brush in cotton
with painted stripes and string whiskers,
1950s. Eeyore, 12 in. by Agnes Brush in
flannel with embroidered sleep eyes, yarn
mane and tail tassel; tail snaps on and off,
1950s.

Agnes Brush Owl, 10 in.
(25 cm) made by Agnes
Brush in the 1950s with
permission of Stephen
Slesinger, Inc. All felt
with hand stitching and
paper hang tag.

Kanga and Roo, 13 in.
(33 cm) & 5 in. (13 cm)
Plush animals made in
1963 by the
Knickerbocker Toy Co.
© Stephen Slesinger.

Rabbit, 11 in. by Agnes
Brush in flannel with
painted eyes and string
whiskers, 1950s.

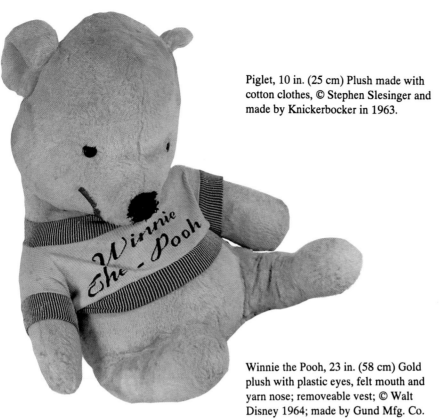

Piglet, 10 in. (25 cm) Plush made with cotton clothes, © Stephen Slesinger and made by Knickerbocker in 1963.

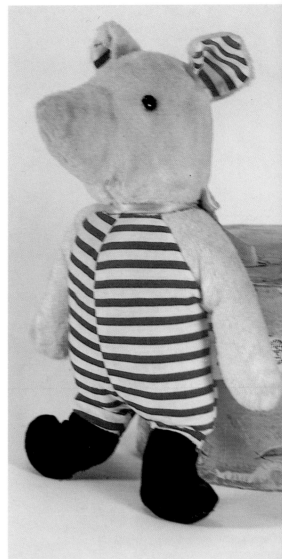

Winnie the Pooh, 23 in. (58 cm) Gold plush with plastic eyes, felt mouth and yarn nose; removeable vest; © Walt Disney 1964; made by Gund Mfg. Co.

Four Poohs, 6 in. (15 cm) in sitting and standing positions, made in velvet by Gund Co., circa 1966, © Disney. *Courtesy Cynthia's Country Store*

Kanga and Roo, 6 in. (15 cm), velvet, © 1964, made in Japan under Walt Disney Copyright. Piglet, 5 in. (13 cm), velvet, © 1966, made in Japan under Walt Disney Copyright. Both animals distributed by Gund. *Courtesy Cynthia's Country Store*

Tigger, 5 in. (13 cm), gold with black striped corduroy and pasted on felt features, made by Gund in 1964 © Walt Disney. Eeyore, 5 in. (13 cm), gray corduroy with felt mane and tail and pasted on felt features; © Walt Disney for Sears stores, circa 1965.

Christopher Robin and Pooh. American artist R. John Wright's faithful rendition of the boy and his bear; © 1986, shown with copy of author's son's first book, 1953.

29

Tigger, 8 1/2 in. (22 cm). Kanga, 9 in. (23 cm). Eeyore, 9 1/2 in. (24 cm). The three remaining animals that are the most well known produced by R. John Wright in 1986 and 1987, © Disney.

Winnie the Pooh, 18 in. (46 cm) by R. John Wright. This is the largest and most desirable of this artist's renditions made in a limited edition of 2500, 1986-1987, © Disney. *Courtesy Cynthia's Country Store*

Winnie the Pooh, 8 in. (20 cm). Piglet, 5 1/2 in. (14 cm). Famous duo produced by R. John Wright in 1985 and 1986; they have become scarce and desirable; Pooh was made in a limited edition of 2,500 and Piglet an edition limited to 1,000, © Disney.

Christopher Robin II, 18 in. Second Christopher Robin by R. John Wright dressed in short pants with suspenders, a t-shirt, raincoat, hat, boots and carrying an umbrella, 1986, 1987 © Disney. Only the first edition is accompanied by Pooh.

Piglet with violets, 7 in. (18 cm), made by
R. John Wright, 1988- 1989 in felt with
glass eyes and wearing a green knit suit,
all jointed, in presentation box. Limited
edition of 2500, © Disney. *Courtesy
Cynthia's Country Store*

Piglet, 9 in. (23 cm), considered the
lifesize model, made by R. John Wright
1986-1987 in felt with bead eyes and
wearing a green suit, all jointed, complete
with hang tag and presentation box in a
limited edition of 1,000 pieces, © Disney

Pocket Piglet, 2 1/2 in., second animal in
the pocket size. Series by R. John Wright,
1994; the rest of the animals will follow,
including Christopher Robin, © Disney.

Winnie the Pooh and chair, 10 in. (25 cm).
A limited edition of 500 made by R. John
Wright for the 1989 Walt Disney World
Convention, © Disney.

Mr. Sander's House and Piglet. R. John Wright's Piglet with violets knocks at the door of Mr. Sander's House. The house is a presentation box that came with the artist's Winnie and his favorite chair, © Disney.

Pocket Pooh, 5 in. (13 cm) © Walt Disney, 1993 issue by R. John Wright, limited to an edition of 3,500 pieces numbered with booklet and in presentation box.

Pooh, 12 in. (31 cm) and 8 in. (20 cm). Made by Anne Wilkinson Designs, © Disney, discontinued in 1993.

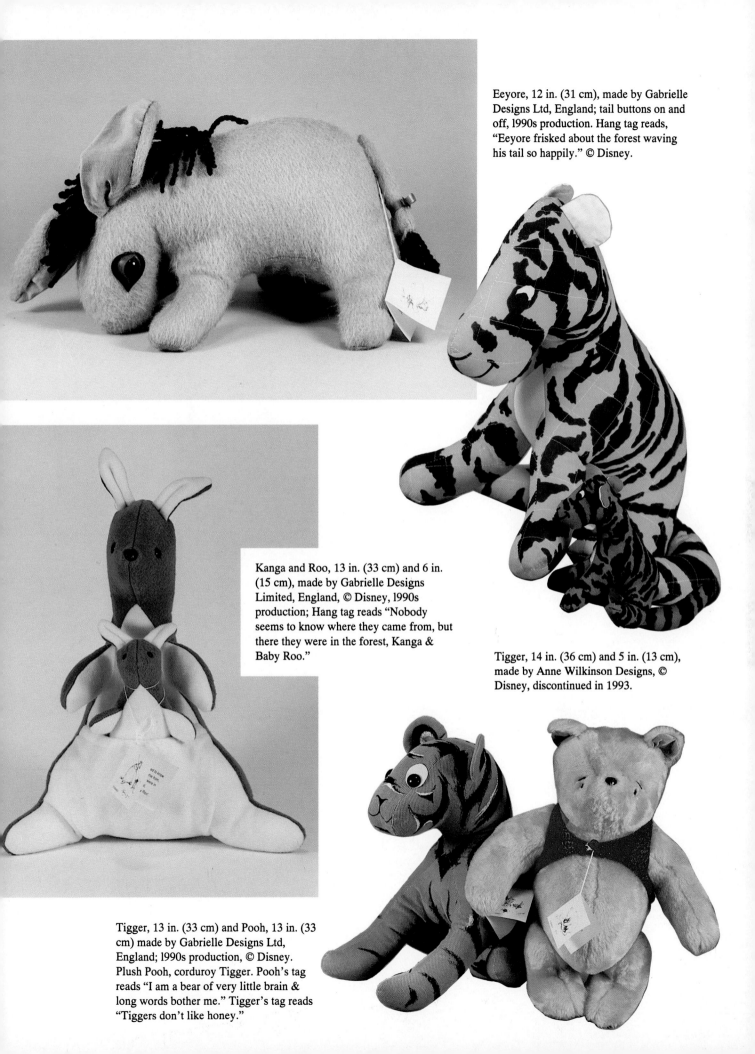

Eeyore, 12 in. (31 cm), made by Gabrielle Designs Ltd, England; tail buttons on and off, 1990s production. Hang tag reads, "Eeyore frisked about the forest waving his tail so happily." © Disney.

Kanga and Roo, 13 in. (33 cm) and 6 in. (15 cm), made by Gabrielle Designs Limited, England, © Disney, l990s production; Hang tag reads "Nobody seems to know where they came from, but there they were in the forest, Kanga & Baby Roo."

Tigger, 14 in. (36 cm) and 5 in. (13 cm), made by Anne Wilkinson Designs, © Disney, discontinued in 1993.

Tigger, 13 in. (33 cm) and Pooh, 13 in. (33 cm) made by Gabrielle Designs Ltd, England; l990s production, © Disney. Plush Pooh, corduroy Tigger. Pooh's tag reads "I am a bear of very little brain & long words bother me." Tigger's tag reads "Tiggers don't like honey."

Eyore, 9 in. (23 cm), velvet with
button-on tail made by Gabrielle in 1993,
© Walt Disney.

Kanga, 10 in. (25 cm), velvet, made by
Gabrielle Designs, 1993, ©Walt Disney.

Piglet, 8 in. (20 cm) made by Gabrielle
Designs Limited, England, © Disney,
1990s production. Piglet carries violets and
the hang tag reads "Piglet had got up early
that morning to pick himself a bunch of
violets."

Pajama Bag/backpack, Plush Eyore made
for the Disney stores
and theme parks, early 1990s, © Disney.
Lori Woo Collection

Piglet, 8 in. (20 cm), plush pink pig found at Disney parks and stores, 1990, © Disney. *Courtesy Cynthia's Country Store*

Piglet, 14 in. (36 cm), unjointed toy made for Sears, circa 1980, © Walt Disney.

Winnie the Pooh hot water bottle, 19 in. (48 cm). Plush Pooh encases a rubber hot bottle, made for Boots stores in England, ©Walt Disney, 1984; shown with plastic presentation bag.

Disneyland '82 Grad Nite Pooh, 14 in. © Walt Disney, made by California Stuffed Toys.

Bear by artist Carol Stewart, 6 in. (15 cm), limited edition of 100 made for the 1990 Walt Disneyworld Convention. *Lori Woo Collection*

Pooh Christmas stocking, 21 in. (53 cm), found at Disney parks and stores, circa 1990, © Disney. *Courtesy Cynthia's Country Store*

Sears Roebuck Poohs. Plush teddies available from the Sears stores ranging in size from 5 in. (13 cm) to 17 in. (43 cm) © Walt Disney. Sears tags, available during the 1970s and 1980s. *Courtesy Cynthia's Country Store*

Miniature Pooh by artist Sherri Dodson, 3 in. (8 cm), 1991. *Courtesy Cynthia's Country Store*

Soon after the books became the most widely read and talked about, in children's literature, rights to reproduce products in all mediums was granted. By 1930, Pooh memorabilia became an industry that continued to grow for the following 60 years and shows no signs of diminishing.

In England, Milne gave the rights to manufacture board games, ceramics, book ends, wallpaper, and wooden figurines. Some of the most elusive pieces of ceramics were made by Ashtead pottery and are, today, extremely rare. The 24 objects were hand painted by Albert Robertson and picture charming arrays of all the characters.

Stephen Slesinger, United States licensee, had many of the china pieces produced in Germany. The ones I've seen have an error in Milne's initials printed A.M. rather than the correct A.A. The bowls are rather heavy and have scenes of wonderful color and enchantment. They are difficult to find, as well, and certainly a thrill when one does. In the 30 years, or more, that Slesinger held the rights, he too introduced a great variety.

Both Methuen and Dutton, publishers, printed all manner of paper items and prints, as well as the books themselves, and continue to do so.

The Walt Disney Corporation's version of Winnie and his friends first appeared in a cartoon and is a far cry from Shepard's interpretation. Children adore him and the prolific output of momentoes can satisfy everyone. The traditional Pooh is also alive and well and still going strong, so whatever your taste or inclination dictates, this bear can fill your life and home endlessly.

Winnie-the-Pooh bowl, divided china dish with three scenes; Marked A.M. Milne (error)/Winnie-the-Pooh/Made in Germany/Richard G. Krueger,NY/Fully protected US Patent Off/Stephen Slesinger Inc; also stamped in green "Bavaria," Schuman, circa 1931.

Child's bowl, 7 1/2 in. (19 cm) diameter. Heavy china featuring scenes involving Christopher Robin, Pooh, Eeyore, Owl, and Mr. Sander's house; marked Germany/ A. M. Milne (error)/ Winnie-the-Pooh/ Made in Germany/ Richard G. Krueger, N.Y./ Fully protected U.S. Pat. Off. /circa 1930. Stephen Slesinger Inc.
Cream pitcher, 3 1/2 in. (9 cm), entitled "Pooh's Dream," a scene from the book; marked Winnie-the-Pooh China/ Design fully protected/ U.S. Pat. Off./Stephen Slesinger Inc/ Made in Bavaria; circa 1930

Winnie the Pooh dish, 8 3/4 in. (22 cm), oval shape, all the characters are having a party, circa 1929, U.S. patent office protected for Stephen Slesinger Inc; charming and rare.

Pooh pitcher, 3 in. (8 cm), yellow ceramic, ear forms the pouring spout, stamped on bottom A.A. Milne/ Winnie the Pooh/ Reg U.S. Pat. Off/ Richard G. Krueger N.Y./ Made in Germany/ Stephen Slesinger Inc., circa 1940.

Wooden Pooh tray, 17 in. (43 cm) x 10 1/2 in. (27 cm). Wooden tray painted yellow with paper overlay showing Christopher Robin, Pooh, and Eeyore in scenes from books, © 1930; marked A M Milne (error) Winnie the Pooh © 1930 Stephen Slesinger Inc. N.Y.

Winnie the Pooh child's gift set containing a feeding spoon made by Community Plate and an embroidered bib which features Rabbit, Kanga, Piglet and Eeyore centered by Pooh and a honey pot. Gift box features colorful graphics, circa 1950, no copyright date.

Queen Holden paper doll, a 1985 repro-
duction of the 1920s issue of Christopher
Robin and Pooh with several outfits; ©
Merrimack Publishing Corp., N. Y.

Framed cut-out paper dolls from an
original set of Winnie the Pooh paper dolls
designed by Queen Holden in the 1920s.

Back of Queen Holden paper doll book.
Kanga, Roo, Piglet, Tigger, and Rabbit;
there are clothes for them as well.

Winnie-the-Pooh puzzle, 8 in. (20 cm) X
10 in. (25 cm). Child' puzzle depicting
Pooh, Piglet, Kanga, and Roo waiting for a
train at the station, 1932, © S. Slesinger,
N.Y.

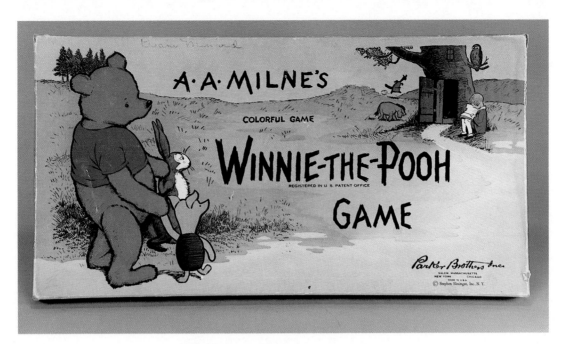

Winnie-the-Pooh game by Parker
Brothers, Inc.

Winnie-the-Pooh puzzle, 8 in. (20 cm) X
10 in. (25 cm). Christopher Robin and
Pooh sailing in Christopher's umbrella,
1932, © S. Slesinger, N.Y.

Winnie-the-Pooh game showing the
playing board, instructions, players and
grab bag of tokens

Framed game pictures from a
Winnie-the-Pooh game of circa 1932 in
which only the painted canvas playing
board was found badly cracked. The intact
areas were resurrected and framed.

Winnie the Pooh record by Decca licensed by Stephen Slesinger Inc. © 1948 featuring songs sung by Frank Luther; includes *Buckingham Palace, Hoppity, The King's Breakfast, The Four Friends, At The Zoo, Halfway Down* and *Vespers* each with verses found in *When We Were Very Young* by Milne and music composed by H. Fraser-Simson. The record cover is decorated with Shepard's drawings.

Record *Two Songs from Winnie-the-Pooh*. A Little Golden record, 45 rpm, circa 1960.

Record of 33 1/3 RPM © 1972 Scholastic Magazine,Inc. *Lori Woo Collection*

Quilt, 35 in. (89 cm) X 46 in (116 cm) embroidered in a Winnie-the- Pooh concept, circa 1940. *Doris Barrows collection*

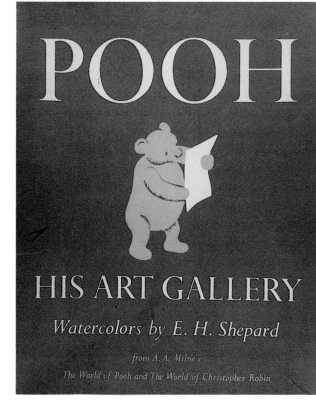

Winnie-the-Pooh needlepoint, 20 in. (51 cm) square. Colorful scenes of Christopher Robin and his friends in a 14 in. (36 cm) circle with designs that approximate Shepard's drawings, circa 1980, ©Disney.

Pooh His Art Gallery, cover of a boxed set of eight prints in large folio size, from colored drawings by E.H. Shepard from *The World of Pooh* and *The World of Christopher Robin*, E.P. Dutton and Company, 1957.

Winnie-the-Pooh prints, each 6 1/2 in. (17 cm) X 8 1/2 in. (22 cm) mounted on cardboard, initialed by the artist Enest Shepard and printed in England, circa 1950: *Christopher Robin has a little something at eleven*, *Christopher Robin's Green Braces*, *Christopher Robin organizes an "Expotition"*, and *What Christopher Robin does in the morning*.

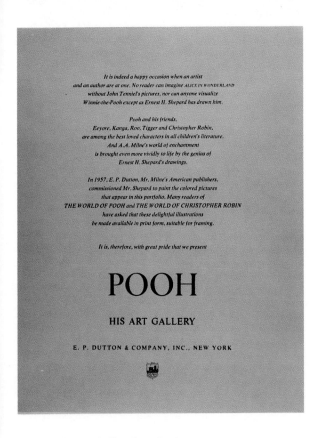

Pooh His Art Gallery introduction paper

Pooh Art Gallery print "Knights and Ladies"

Pooh Art Gallery print "Pooh and Christopher Robin rest in an enchanted place on the very top of the forest."

Pooh Art Gallery print "Tigger and Roo are out on a limb."

Pooh Art Gallery print "Pooh's party"

Pooh Art Gallery print "An anxious moment--Pooh and his friends watch for Eeyore to float by"

Pooh Art Gallery print "Pooh does his stoutness exercises."

Pooh Art Gallery print "Pooh and Piglet look on as Eeyore tries to put the balloon into the pot."

Pooh Figurine; ceramic; styrofoam
balloon with bee; retains original hand
tag; made by Enesco; circa 1965. ©
Walt Disney. *Lori Woo Collection*

Piglet; 2 1/2 in; by R. John Wright; part
of a set that includes Pocket Pooh in a
limited edition of 500 pieces; exclusively for F A O Schwarz; in this
version Piglet's suit has sleeves and he
wears a scarf; 1994; © *Walt Disney.*

Pooh Art Gallery Print "Tigger cannot
answer Pooh and Piglet; his mouth is full
of acorns."

Heffalump; 6 in; velveteen with felt
features; made by Gund; circa 1965 ©
W. Disney. *Lori Woo Collection*

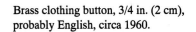

Winnie the Pooh stamps. British stamp that was part of a series commemorating the Year of The Child in 1979. Grenada stamp featuring Disney characters. Pooh was part of the collection. © W. Disney. Seven stamps issued by Anguilla in 1982 to celebrate the anniversary of A.A. Milne's birth.© W. Disney.

Lesotho stamp for Christmas, 1985 combining Pooh and friends with a quote from Mark Twain, "Boston is a state of mind." © Walt Disney.

Brass clothing button, 3/4 in. (2 cm), probably English, circa 1960.

Pendant of turquoise enamel, seed pearls and 18 k gold with a place for a photograph insert. In the 1990s when this was on the market, a pencil sketch of Pooh was inserted.

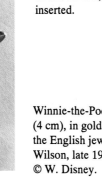

Winnie-the-Pooh's head brooch, 1 1/2 in (4 cm), in gold, red and black diamenté by the English jewelry designers Butler and Wilson, late 1980s and 1990s production. © W. Disney.

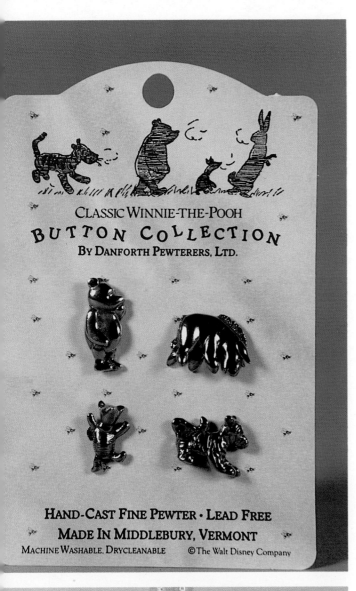

Winnie-the-Pooh pewter buttons of Pooh, Eeyore, Piglet and Tigger; made by the Danforth Pewterers Ltd, Vermont, © Walt Disney Co., 1990 production.

Child's dress of cotton blend fabric with a print featuring Pooh, Eeyore, Tigger and Piglet, size 5, made for Sears Roebuck Co, ©Walt Disney, 1980s. The dress is shown on a 24 in. (61 cm) Steiff teddy bear, circa 1928.

Sterling silver pendant by a California jewelry artist, circa 1986. At the top is "Mr. Sander's" tree house and the charms suspended below represent Christopher Robin, Pooh, Eeyore, Piglet and other characters from the Pooh series books.

Winnie-the-Pooh cutouts © Walt Disney, date unknown. The lithographed paper is mounted on hardboard as a decoration for a child's room; holes on the back are for hanging.

Enamel boxes, 1 1/8 in. (3 cm) X 2 1/4 in. (8 cm). Decorative trinket boxes made in England by Crummles with E.H. Shepard designs, 1990s, © Berne convention.

Colored print, 12 X 15 in., available at the Pooh Corners Gift Shop, 1993.

Wrist watch with silhouette drawing made by Apollo for England and other European countries. Discontinued in 1990; © Disney
Lori Woo Collection

Winnie-the-Pooh table model telephone, 14 in., with push button dial. Winnie holds the hand set; made by American TeleCommunications Corp., © 1964 Walt Disney.

Ceramic mug made by Willitts in 1989 for U.S.distribution; © Disney *Lori Woo Collection*

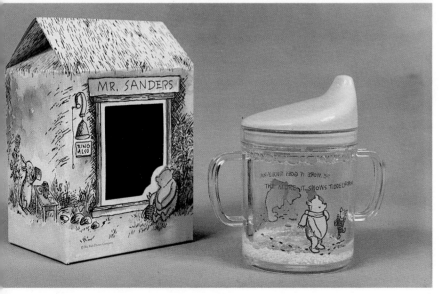

Two handled training mug made by Selandia in 1991; © Disney *Lori Woo Collection*

Christopher Robin and Pooh switchplate made of pewter and distributed in 1989; © Disney *Lori Woo Collection*

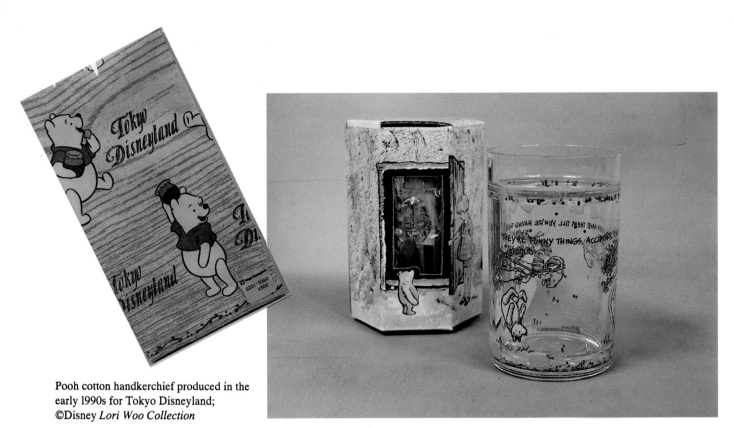

Pooh cotton handkerchief produced in the early 1990s for Tokyo Disneyland; ©Disney *Lori Woo Collection*

Winnie the Pooh tumbler made by Selandia in 1991 for distribution in the United States; © Disney *Lori Woo Collection*

Vinyl covered fabric key ring by Anne Wilkinson Designs Ltd. Sold in England in the early 1990s; © Disney *Lori Woo Collection*

Satin ball by Hallmark; 1979; © Disney *Lori Woo Collection*

Pooh back pack of pink nylon manufactured by Copywrite Stationary Ltd. in the
early 1990s; © Disney. Sold in England.
Lori Woo Collection

Disney wristwatch with leather band
impressed with bees; bees also circle
Pooh's head when watch is running, 1990;
© Disney *Courtesy Cynthia's Country
Store*

Painted metal tray, Willitts design, 1989;
© Disney *Lori Woo Collection*

Animation cel "The Many Adventures of
Winnie The Pooh." © Disney *Lori Woo
Collection*

Ceramic bear ornament by Hallmark, 1991, © Disney *Courtesy Cynthias Country Store*

Winnie the Pooh china mug with book characters and Christopher Robin on the presentation box, l99l; © Disney *Courtesy Cynthia's Country Store*

Winnie the Pooh jumping jack, 6 in. (15 cm), Walt Disney Productions for Christmas of 1991, paper over hardboard with pull string to articulate limbs; © Disney *Courtesy Cynthia's Country Store*

Winnie the Pooh writing set with ten
sheets of paper and envelopes; © Disney.
Hunkydory Designs Limited, made in
England, 1990.

Winnie the Pooh greeting cards which
open to become dimentional; Hunkydory
Designs, England, 1987; © Disney

Winnie and Piglet walk off

Chapter Two

Raggedy Ann

Johnny Gruelle And Raggedy Ann

Faceless. Faded. Showing the ravages of time. That is how the limp rag doll appeared as she was lifted from the depths of an attic barrel. The child, who had been playing in the cosy garret, looked upon the relic she had discovered with tender pity. Clearly it cried for help and surely, the child thought, her clever father could attend to the dolls needs. Running to share her new found treasure with him she learned it had been made for her grandmother by her great grandmother. Dolly was very old indeed, yet retained a warm charm that appealed to the little girl who clasped it.

The father set to his task sewing on shoe buttons for eyes and painting a smiling mouth beneath a triangular nose. Father and child gazed at the remarkable transformation and were delighted. Yet wait. Something was missing. Ah yes; everyone needs a heart to be truly brought to life. So once more the brush was dipped into the red paint and a heart with the inscription "I love you" was drawn on the chest. The man was John Barton Gruelle, the child his only daughter Marcella, and the doll ultimately became known to generations of children as "Raggedy Ann"

Johnny entered the world at Christmas time in the 1880s, one of three children born to Richard and Alice Gruelle. Although he made his debut in Arcola, Illinois, his parents relocated to Indianapolis, Indiana before the chimes rang in the New Year.

His father, Richard Gruelle, gained prominence as a landscape and portrait painter, thus the children were raised in an artistic environment. John's brother, Justin, became an illustrator, his sister Prudence a writer and Johnny himself combined both talents. All three children were encouraged to produce all varieties of art work and Johnny never envisioned any other career. He was completely self taught having declined art lessons, including those offered by his father. Formal education ceased, according to rumor, when he refused to recite an assigned poem. Perhaps this seemingly stubborn streak is just the mark of an artistic personality marching to the tune of a different drummer. When one has a burning thirst for individuality and a consummate passion to release this energy, it cannot be quenched by conformist standards.

Sheet Music; *Raggedy Ann;* from the 1923 Broadway musical "The Stepping Stones;" music by Jerome Kern, lyrics by Ann Caldwell. *Bonnie and Larry Vaughan Collection*

Quacky Doodles And Danny Daddles; 8 1/2 in; wooden Mama and Papa ducks; Doodle's bonnet is calico; Schoenhut for P.F. Volland Co. Danny has tag on bottom left foot with patent date (and design date of Sept. 1915); characters created by Gruelle. *Bonnie and Larry Vaughan Collection*

Here is a man grasping destiny in his own hands, turning his back on academia and carving out a living in a highly prolific manner. With determined ambition and belief in his own talents he reached for the stars achieving his goals one by one. How ironic it is to realize that his greatest legacy came not completely from his innate gifts but, as we shall see, a direct result of a personal tragedy.

Although Johnny became best known as a writer and illustrator of childrens' books, his career began as a cartoonist starting with employment, at age 19, with the *Indianapolis People*. By 1902 he was working for two other Indianapolis newspapers, followed by a move in 1905 to the *Cleveland Press*. His longest stint as a cartoonist was with the New York Herald where he stayed for seven years.

It was during the *Herald* tenure that he originated the comic strip "Brutus." In 1910 he won a contest, sponsored by the *Herald*, over 500 other entrants. The strip "Mr. Twee Deedle" ran in the Sunday comics until 1921. It was so popular that even the Steiff Company in Germany produced his likeness in a charming felt doll. Until that time his work included satirical looks at politics, sports, and the weather, although he always found a fascination with fairy tales and yearned to do some first class renderings. "Mr Twee Deedle" started him on that path, for this character was beautifully honed and led to other fantasies as his life unfolded.

John worked swiftly and unerringly; at one point telling nine stories into a dictaphone during an evening at home and ultimately selling them for nine hundred dollars. By this time he was a family man with a daughter, Marcella, the first child born of his union with Myrtle Swann. His son, Worth, followed in his fathers footsteps eventually illustrating Raggedy books after John's death. Another son, Richard, fondly recalls childhood memories of himself, Worth, a dog and his parents spending two years traveling West. If this seems a rather prolonged vacation one must remember that Gruelle's occupation allowed him to do this. He wrote and drew as the family journeyed, staying at farms along the way.

This idyllic, rather nomadic, existance occurred several years after tragedy struck the family. In 1916 Marcella, his beloved daughter, died after a long illness, resulting from a contaminated vaccination needle. The loss of a child is the cruelest of life's slings and arrows and yet John managed to immortalize Marcella in a manner that has brought immeasurable joy to others. One can envision his tear filled eyes gazing at the rag doll that Marcella had found and even in grief his fertile imagination taking flight. In 1918 the first book *Raggedy Ann Stories* was published as a poignant memento to the little girl who never lived to read it.

The Gruelle family massed together to fashion several rag dolls to help advertise the volume in store window displays. John and his brother Justin painted the faces, sister Prudence rubber stamped the bodies with pertinent data and young Worth bought candy hearts inscribed "I love you" to be sewn inside the chest. Oddly enough John had patented the doll in September 1915, a clear indication that he was protecting his rights and he had future plans.

The dolls proved so popular that it was soon determined the family could not handle the response. A large order from the Marshall Field Co. tipped the balance and P. F. Volland, the books publisher, was licensed to produce the dolls as well. Volland Raggedies are the most coveted today. They do not follow the patent design but presumably the family efforts did not either. The patent example wears a flower trimmed bonnet and a puffy apron while the Volland Raggedy is closer to what we are currently accustomed to. They were made in a size of 15 or 16 inches, had thick dark brown yarn hair and the feet turned outward. The general appearance of each face is the same, but subtle variations occur and these nuances should be noted by studying the photographs.

The candy hearts tended to melt and were abandoned in favor of wooden ones. These can sometimes be felt through the fabric on the early models. Eventually a heart and inscription were drawn directly on the chest in the manner of Marcella's doll. This familiar logo became a beloved symbol recognized by children the world over.

Georgene Ann; 50 in; rare store display; black outlined nose; original clothes; 1938. *Judith Armistead Collection*

By 1920 the popularity of Raggedy Ann had risen to soaring heights and the public clamored for more. A sequel called *Raggedy Andy Stories* made a debut, soon followed by a Volland cloth likeness. The boy's confirmation follows Ann's and he is costumed in blue trousers that button onto a plaid shirt. A neck bow and a sailor cap complete his attire.

John continued to write and draw in his customary fertile manner. In one ten day period he managed to illustrate a Raggedy book in color and produce 30 illustrations and drawings for two publications. All this effort to ensure a family vacation would proceed as scheduled. He continued the Raggedy saga by writing sequel after sequel, keeping them in boxes and then seeing one in publication nearly every year until his death.

1926 saw the emergence of a book, followed by a doll that still captures collectors imagination. *Beloved Belindy* was described as a black mammy who was fat and cheerful with a broad happy smile. As in the premise of all the stories, the dolls caper and prance at night when the household sleeps or during the day when no one is at home. The Volland Company produced this image, as well, and this charming doll is now quite rare and highly desired.

Marcella, published in 1929 by M. A. Donahue and Co., is John's lasting memorial to his dear daughter. The cover, showing the curly headed blond child with Ann and Andy surrounded by vines and blooms, is perhaps the loveliest rendition of all.

John Gruelle's talents encompassed an artistic vein that extended beyond the written word and drawings. The year 1930 saw a collaboration with William H. Woodin, president of the American Can and Foundry Corp, in putting his stories into songs. The ensuing book *Raggedy Ann's Sunny Songs* received wide critical attention. He often sat at the piano composing melodies for his tales and this in turn led to an association with John E. Mahon for the musical comedy stage.

In 1931 a move to Florida, partly for health reasons, took place. He continued, however, his life's work and, all told, published fifteen other children's books in addition to the Raggedies. After his death in 1938 of heart disease, a wealth of other unpublished material became one of his legacies. Howard Cox, publisher, and the Gruelles formed the Johnny Gruelle Co, for the purpose of issuing new material and consolidating the old. In 1961 Mr. Cox is quoted in *The New York World Telegram* describing Gruelle as a man to whom children were drawn like a magnet. It may also be said that children continue to be drawn to him via his lasting heritage, Raggedy Ann. No doll, before or since, has captured the hearts of so many for the piquant face appeals to young and old alike. It is sweet without being simpering, happy without guise and, above all, soft so that even the youngest child can feel safe in a warm embrace.

Georgene awake/asleep Ann; 13 in; of particular interest since legs are solid mustard color rather than traditional stripes; produced during WWII when there was a shortage of materials; circa 1941. *Bonnie and Larry Vaughan Collection*

Sheet Music; *No Speak 'Merican;* from Paramount's 1941 color cartoon *Raggedy Ann and Raggedy Andy. Bonnie and Larry Vaughan Collection*

Boxed set of three puzzles; 9 in X 12 in (each); Milton Bradley; 1954; one shown. *Bonnie and Larry Vaughan Collection*

Georgene Ann; 15 in; tin eyes; red paint dress; rick rack trim on apron; circa 1960. *Judith Armitstead Collection*

Raggedy Ann; 25 in; notable for unusual two-tone yarn hair; Knickerbocker; 1960s. *Judith Armitstead Collection*

Raggedy Arthur; 12 in; toy dog made by Knickerbocker in 1965. *Bonnie and Larry Vaughan Collection*

Watering can; 9 in high (including handle); Bobbs-Merrill Co. 1973. *Bonnie and Larry Vaughan Collection*

Ann and Andy Shoe Shine Kit; brushes have dolls heads with roll around eyes; Griffin shoe polish and other accessories; *Bobbs-Merrill,* 1974. *Bonnie and Larry Vaughan Collection*

Volume By Volume

Johnny Gruelle, man of many talents, saw his books printed by a variety of publishers in editions that can be counted in the millions. Raggedy Ann and her troop of colorful friends were issued by P.F. Volland, M.A. Donahue, J. Gruelle Co, McLoughlin, Myrtle Gruelle Co, and Bobbs Merrill.

The Titles

1. *Raggedy Ann Stories*
2. *Raggedy Andy Stories*
3. *Raggedy Ann and Andy's Very Own Fairy Tales*
4. *The Camel with the Wrinkled Knees*
5. *Raggedy Ann's Wishing Pebbles*
6. *Raggedy Ann and Andy Alphabet Numbers*
7. *Beloved Belindy*
8. *Raggedy Ann and The Paper Dragon*
9. *Raggedy Ann's Fairy Tales*
10. *Raggedy Ann's Magical Wishes*
11. *Marcella*
12. *Raggedy Ann In the Deep, Deep Woods*
13. *Raggedy Ann In Cookieland*
14. *Raggedy Ann's Lucky Pennies*
15. *Raggedy Ann's Alphabet Book*
16. *Raggedy Ann and The Left Handed Safety Pin*
17. *Raggedy Ann in The Magic Book*
18. *Raggedy Ann and The Golden Butterfly*
19. *Raggedy Andy In the Garden*
20. *Raggedy Andy Goes Sailing*
21. *Raggedy Ann and Andy And The Nice Fat Policeman*
22. *Raggedy Ann and Betsy Bonnet String*
23. *Raggedy Ann in The Snow White Castle*
24. *Raggedy Ann and The Hobby Horse*
25. *Raggedy Ann and The Happy Meadow*
26. *Raggedy Ann and The Wonderful Witch*
27. *Raggedy Ann Helps Grandpa Hoppergrass*
28. *Raggedy Ann and The Laughing Brook*
29. *Raggedy Ann at The End Of The Rainbow*
30. *Raggedy Ann and Andy's Friendly Fairies*
31. *Raggedy Ann and The Golden Ring*

Although the bulk of the books were self illustrated, some of the manuscripts found after his death saw his son Worth and his brother Justin taking on the task and following John's style remarkably well. Since the 1940s other editions in larger paper format have been printed with drawings by other artists. Golden Books and Grosset and Dunlap have used June Goldsborough, while Perks and The American Crayon Co. ,have featured Mary and Wallace Stover.

The copyrights have gone through numerous changes with a myriad of publishers and a diversity of artesans taking up the torch.

1. *Raggedy Ann and Andy*. Saalfield 1944, illustrated by Julian Wehr.
2. *Raggedy Ann and The Slippery Slide*. Saalfield 1947, illustrated by Ethel Hays.
3. *Raggedy Ann's Mystery*. Saalfield 1947, illustrated by Ethel Hays.
4. *Raggedy Ann's Adventure*. Saalfield 1947, illustrated by Ethel Hays.
5. *Raggedy Ann at the End of the Rainbow*. Saalfield 1947, illustrated by Ethel Hays.

Movie Poster; 27 X 41 in; a musical full length cartoon movie produced in 1977 by 20th Century Fox; entitled *Raggedy Ann And Andy–A Musical Adventure;* a video version is available in some stores. *Bonnie and Larry Vaughan Collection*

6. *Raggedy Ann's Merriest Christmas.* Wonder Books 1952, illustrated by T. Sinnickson.

7. *Raggedy Andy's Surprise.* Wonder Books 1952, illustrated by T. Sinnickson.

8. *Raggedy Ann's Tea Party.* Wonder Books 1954, illustrated by George and Irma Wilde.

Although John left behind a wealth of material the clamor for more adventures prompted other writers to emulate him. Thus we find not only additional artists but other authors as well continuing where Gruelle stopped.

1. *Raggedy Ann Stories.* Western Publishing 1969, by Barbara S. Hazen.
2. *Raggedy Ann and Fido.* Western Publishing 1969, by Janet Fulton.
3. *Raggedy Ann: A Thank You, Please, and I Love You Book.* Western Publishing 1970, by Nora Smaridge.
4. *Raggedy Ann and The Daffy Taffy Pull.* Hallmark 1972, by Dean Walley.
5. *Raggedy Ann and the Sad Glad Days.* Western Publishing 1973, by Mary Carey.
6. *Raggedy Ann and Raggedy Andy Book.* Western Publishing 1973, by Jan Sukus.
7. *Raggedy Andy: The I Can Do It, You Can Do It Book.* Western Publishing 1973, by Nora Smaridge.
8. *Raggedy Ann and Andy and the Rainy Day Circus.* Western Publishing 1973, by B.S. Hazen.
9. *Raggedy Ann and Andy's Cookbook.* Bobbs-Merrill 1975, by Nika Hazelton.
10. *Raggedy Ann and Andy's Green Thumb Book.* Bobbs-Merrill 1975. by Alix R. Nelson.
11. *Raggedy Ann's Sweet and Dandy Sugar Candy Fragrance Book.* Western Publishing 1976, by Patricia Thackray.
12. *Raggedy Ann and Andy.* Bobbs-Merrill 1977, by Kathleen N. Daly.

This enduring soft doll has also been the basis of other artistic venues. In 1940 Paramount Pictures released a movie entitled "Raggedy Ann," Johnny Gruelle co-produced "Raggedy Ann and Andy Time No. 1," and an animated version, "Raggedy Ann and Andy," with screenplay by Patricia Thackray and Max Wilk was the offspring of Bobbs-Merrill in 1977. *The Camel with the Wrinkled Knees* prompted Marie Agnes Foley in 1940 to write a fantasy play for Dramatists Publishing.

In recent years other formats have been developed. Because Raggedy Ann's appeal has not diminished we can be assured that future generations will be able to experience the delight of reveling in the tales of a wonderful rag doll.

Little Brown Bear; 13 in; Teddy produced to emulate the bear in the 1920 book by Gruelle of the same title; made by House of Nisbet, England in 1987; limited to 5,000 although only about 1,000 were actually made; came with booklet and signed by John's son Worth Gruelle. *Bonnie and Larry Vaughan Collection*

All original Raggedy Andy and Ann, 15 in. (38 cm), by Volland, circa 1920, they have shoebutton eyes, painted features, toes pointed outward and original clothes. Ann has dark hair and a wooden heart sewn inside the body.

Raggedy Ann and "Company"

The P. F. Volland Co. was the first licensed organization to create and distribute a Raggedy Ann doll. This version is sweet indeed with her shoe button eyes and smiling mouth. The nose, normally outlined in black, occasionally is not in evidence whether by fading or perhaps a slip-up in production. Compared to the hand, the thumb appears outsized and could be a useful identification tool. Rather thick yarn hair in a dark brown hue differs from the orange or red we are accustomed to seeing. Red and white striped legs ending in black, outward turned feet, and dressed in dainty prints of the period add to her winsome appearance.

Raggedy Andy came upon the scene two years later and, like Ann, subtle variations in eyelashes, noses and mouths can be discerned. Andy's hair is more auburn and generally his shirt is plaid rather than checked. Blue trousers button onto the shirt both front and back and buttons also decorate the pants on the sides of the bottom. A blue and white sailor cap sits atop his head while a small neck bow completes his costuming.

At some point in the decade, following the 1926 publication of *Beloved Belindy* her likeness was also created as a Volland doll. The dark brown fabric is enhanced by sewn on white button eyes beneath white painted brows, and a wide smiling mouth with marks designating teeth. Her red and white striped legs end in red feet that matches the kerchief tied around her head with the knot in front. The crimson dress-top has a printed skirt overlaid by a lace trimmed apron.

An appealing selection of Anns made by Volland, circa 1920. Each expression is slightly different and they have differently printed dresses. *Candy Brainard collection*

Note the different body styles on these Ann dolls by Volland and the different widths of stripes on their legs, circa 1918-1925. *Candy Brainard collection*

Talking Quartz Alarm Clock; plastic; features Ann, Andy and Arthur; made in Hong Kong; circa 1975. *Bonnie and Larry Vaughan Collection*

Original Beloved Belindy, 15 in. (38 cm) by P.F. Volland Co., 1926, a very hard doll to find, here shown with the book that featured her. *Candy Brainard Collection*

The Volland Company continued to publish the books as they were presented. These first editions were dust jacketed and marketed in presentation boxes, and to find copies in this original condition is a joyful experience. The Company ceased operations in 1934 and the torch has been passed to many enterprises in the subsequent years.

The firm next licensed to make the dolls was the Exposition Toy and Doll Company who operated from late 1934 until the middle of 1935. Their example retained the brown hair, but the eyes were printed in pie shape and the red dot disappeared from the center of the black line mouth. Since their tenure was so short it is extremely difficult to locate a sample of their product. They were forced to abandon their ship for a pirate was on the loose and doing very well with their illegal business.

Mollye's Doll Outfitters patented their version of Ann and Andy in 1935. Mollye Goldman did this without the Gruelle s permission and a court battle ensued lasting until 1938. Since the design was somewhat diverse, using multicolored legs, side glancing eyes and an organdy pinafore she thought she was within her rights. Still, when advised of the illegality of her actions, she continued production until she was forced to stop. The dolls were 15 to 20 in. and identified by marks on the torso. Mollye also produced 14 inch "Babies" with shorter noses and, in the case of Ann, the back of the head is made from the same print as her dress. These particular dolls carry no identifying labels.

In 1938 the Gruelle s issued permission to Georgene Novelties Co. Inc. of New York to begin manufacturing. During the 25 year span that this enterprise produced the dolls various alterations and tags were employed. Six different mouth shapes were used (although all of them retained the red center,) eyelashes varied in width, and the first tin eyes were later replaced by plastic. The rather long triangular noses were first outlined in black and they evolved into shorter versions with outlines eliminated. Georgene dolls have seams at the center of both arms and legs to simulate elbows and knees. Except for the awake/asleep dolls, all feet face forward. Ordinarily the legs retain the traditional red and white stripes, but the occasional diversity of fabric use has been found. Four different tags were employed, varying during different years of production, and these were all sewn into side seams.

Raggedy Andy, 26 in. (66 cm) with a cotton muslin body, pale gold yarn hair, shoe button eyes, and embroidered nose, mouth, eyebrows and three lower lashes. He wears cotton shirt, trousers, hat and striped socks and alligator printed shoes. Stamped on his chest is "Little Eva's Washable Toys," circa 1925. *Judith Armitstead Collection*

Georgene made a Beloved Belindy as well. She compares somewhat in appearance to Volland's except that the body fabric is a lighter brown and the dress bodice is trimmed by four painted buttons. The lace that adorns the more opaque cotton of the apron,and trims the neck and sleeves,is of the eyelet variety. Manufacturing data is normally stamped on the back of the head, but a rarer version shows the stamp on the torso (see illustration.)

The *Camel with the Wrinkled Knees*, first published in 1924, saw his counterpart made by Georgene as well. This somewhat elusive creature is fashioned in a rather cartoon-like manner and is a pleasing addition to a collection.

In 1962 The Knickerbocker Toy Co. made an offer so lucrative the Gruelle s decided not to renew the Georgene contract. During Knickerbockers 20 year span various alterations marked their examples as well, chiefly the orange hair changing to red. Mouths and eyelashes varied , but basically the doll remained constant, although many more sizes were introduced. Ten different labels appeared and they can be found on the clothes rather than the body.

Their version of Beloved Belindy is still light brown, but the eyes are off center plastic over white circles and the teeth have been sacrificed. The red top is sometimes polka dotted as is the skirt, although a print is sometimes used. The apron is bias bound rather than laced trimmed and identification is by a paper hang tag. She originally came in a presentation box as did most of the Anns and Andys.

Knickerbocker's camel is a velour-like fabric, 11 inches tall, and with a felt harness. This company is the first to really diversify and make an enormous variety of dolls and related accessories. These include sleeping bags, talking models, puppets, pillows and even a Raggedy Arthur dog complete with yarn hair.

The Applause Company began as a division of Knickerbocker in 1979, producing Raggedies from 1981 until 1983. They embroidered the faces and only made four sizes of 12, 17, 25 and 36 inches. A merging of Applause with Wallace-Berrie in the early 1980s resulted in the licensing of Raggedy taken over by the Hasbro Company. They continue this operation to the present.

Over the years other companies made dolls that, while not strictly Raggedies,carry the essence and they should not be overlooked. The American Toy and Novelty Company's output have faces of oil cloth and use a variety of striped legs. The varied outfits can be quite interesting and if a tag is present it reads "I'm a Buddy Huggable Nursery Pet, American Toy and Novelty Mfg. Co." Unfortunately a definitive date cannot be given or the length of production.

Around 1920, a 25-inch model appeared that resembled a bed doll. They are sometimes stamped in blue on both the front and the back, reading "Little Eva's Washable Toys." The muslin bodies have shoe button eyes surrounded by eyelashes in a starburst design. Triangular noses and a smiling mouth complete the face that is enhanced by rather wild hair in an unraveled yarn. The girl doll has a wooden heart encased in the body.

Many home made dolls were fashioned by expert sewers, some via printed patterns and others by artists of extreme talent.

Most follow the traditional design while others are customized by clever additions and embellishments. Several artists are currently offering their wares and these are very appealing indeed. They can be a very wonderful addition to a collection and add an extra fillip of delight.

Another version of Little Eva's Raggedy Ann, 24 in. (61 cm), with a different dress print and smooth leather shoes, unmarked, circa 1925. *Judith Armitstead Collection*

Little Eva's Ann and Andy, circa 1925.

Raggedy Ann, 26 in. (66 cm). This charming muslin doll has embroidered features including ten eyelashes in a starburst design around shoe button eyes and curly yarn hair. She is wearing nicely made white pantaloons and petticoat, and a white apron over a print dress, alligator printed leather shoes and striped socks. She has a wooden heart with scalloped edges that can be felt under the chest fabric and she is stamped "Little Eva's Washable Toys," circa 1925. *Judith Armitstead Collection*

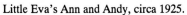

Yet another set of Little Eva's Raggedy Ann and Andy dolls, 24 in. (61 cm). All of the Little Eva examples have been found in the New England area, circa 1925. *Phyllis Kransberg Collection*

Little Eva's Ann, 26 in. (66 cm). This charming doll was fashioned in the manner of a "bed doll" popular in the period circa 1925. It has a muslin body, cotton filling, raveled yarn hair, shoe button eyes, embroidered features, and a replaced dress; no marks. *Candy Brainard Collection*

Raggedy Ann, 21 in. (53 cm) by Mollye's Doll Outfitters, all original, circa 1935.

Markings on the front of Mollye's Raggedy Ann.

This extremely elusive Raggedy Ann doll was made by Exposition Doll and Toy Co. for less than one year from late 1934 until the middle of 1935. Note the tagged dress. *Candy Brainard Collection*

Raggedy Andy, 14 in. (36 cm) by Mollye's Outfitters; all original except for replaced hat, 1935-1938. *Candy Brainard collection*

Unmarked Raggedy Ann, 22 in. (56 cm) made by Mollye's Outfitters with a wooden heart that originally was in the chest but has shifted to the back and may be felt through the fabric. The clothes are all original, circa 1935.

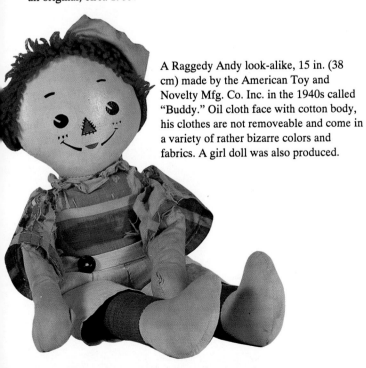

A Raggedy Andy look-alike, 15 in. (38 cm) made by the American Toy and Novelty Mfg. Co. Inc. in the 1940s called "Buddy." Oil cloth face with cotton body, his clothes are not removeable and come in a variety of rather bizarre colors and fabrics. A girl doll was also produced.

Mollye's Doll Outfitters mark on Raggedy Andy. *Candy Brainard collection*

69

Another Beloved Belindy, 18 in. (46 cm) by Georgene Novelties, all original and in pristine condition, circa 1938.

Raggedy Andy, 19 in. (48 cm) made by Georgene, circa 1938, whose earliest tag is sewn on the body, all original.

Beloved Belindy identification stamped on the body. This stamp position is believed to be older and a more rare placement than on the head.

Beloved Belindy, 18 in. (46 cm) by Georgene Novelties; original except missing the apron. Indentification is stamped on her head under the bandana, circa 1938.

Raggedy Ann, 19 in. (48 cm), made by Georgene circa 1938. This has the earliest tag sewn on the body; clothes not original.

Raggedy Ann and Raggedy Andy, 32 in. (81 cm), an impressive size and all original. Note the black outlined noses, circa 1940 Shown with a J. G. C. bean bag Raggedy Ann, circa 1940, and a little Georgene Raggedy Andy, 15 in. (38 cm). This little Andy is the two-faced, awake/asleep version with a black outlined nose, circa 1940. *Candy Brainard collection*

Raggedy Ann and Raggedy Andy, 19 in. (48 cm) by Georgene with outlined noses and all original except that Andy is missing his hat, circa 1940. *Candy Brainard collection*

Raggedy Andy and Raggedy Ann Awake/Asleep: 12 in (31 cm) Georgene Novelties; circa l940; all original black outlined nose; reverse of head shows her awake.

Raggedy Andy and Raggedy Ann, 15 in. (38 cm) by Georgene with awake/asleep faces, black outlined noses, and original clothes, circa 1940. *Candy Brainard collection*

Raggedy Ann and Raggedy Andy, 13 in. (33 cm) made by Georgene in the 1940s and tagged on the body. The clothes are original.

Georgene Awake/Asleep Raggedy Ann, 12 in. (31 cm), all original with an unusual star printed dress and black outlined nose, circa 1940.

Raggedy Ann, 22 in. (56 cm) by Georgene. Note the unusual feet made of fabric that matches her dress, circa 1940. *Candy Brainard collection*

Awake/Asleep Raggedy Ann, 15 in. (38 cm) by Georgene with two faces, black outlined nose, all original, circa 1940. *Candy Brainard collection*

Two Raggedy Anns, 20 in. (51 cm) by Georgene. Note the curved shape of the mouth and the paler, more orange hair than later examples, circa 1940.

Raggedy Ann, 15 in. (38 cm) by Georgene, 1947, tagged BMC Inc. Note Ann's horse-print dress. *Candy Brainard collection*

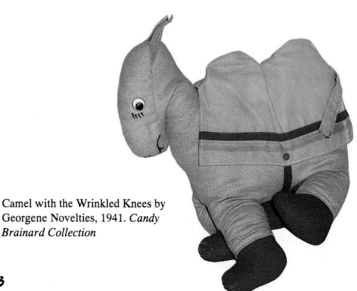

Camel with the Wrinkled Knees by Georgene Novelties, 1941. *Candy Brainard Collection*

Raggedy Ann by Georgene, 20 in. (51 cm) wearing a dress with a pretty print and a replaced apron, 1950s.

Beloved Belindy, 16 in. (41 cm) made by Knickerbocker in 1965 but had a short production as a result of the Civil Rights movement in the United States, all original.

Beloved Belindy, 29 in. (74 cm). This hand-made doll, probably of the 1950s era, is well constructed and captures the essence of commercial products with a painted face with button eyes and a good choice of cotton fabrics for the body and clothes.

Beloved Belindy, 15 in. (38 cm) by Knickerbocker, circa 1965, mint in box with original paper tag. *Candy Brainard collection*

A group of Raggedy Anns and Raggedy Andys by Georgene in sizes ranging from 14 in. (36 cm) to 20 in. (51 cm). Andy on the front left and Ann on the front right are the earliest and they both have shoe button eyes. Note the early Andy's outlined nose and the charming print of early Ann's dress, circa 1938 - 1950.

Raggedy Ann and Raggedy Andy, 14 in. (36 cm) by Knickerbocker in original boxes with heart label still intact; note turquoise color of box, circa 1960. *Candy Brainard collection*

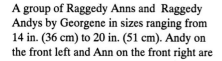

Musical Raggedy Ann and Raggedy Andy, 15 in. (38 cm) by Knickerbocker both retain original paper labels, 1966 by Myrtle Gruelle. *Candy Brainard collection*

Talking Raggedy Ann, 17 in. (43 cm) by Knickerbocker, mint in box, circa 1965. Ann talks via pull string mechanism. *Candy Brainard collection*

Raggedy Ann and Raggedy Andy, 18 in.
(46 cm) by Knickerbocker, circa 1960, in
original and unusual boxes. *Candy
Brainard collection*

Raggedy Ann pillow, 10 in. (25 cm)
possibly made from a kit, no tag, probably
Bobbs/Merrill Company, 1960s

Graduated sizes of miniature Raggedy Ann
and Raggedy Andy dolls by
Knickerbocker, the largest is 5 in. (13 cm),
1970s *Candy Brainard collection*

A quartet of different era Raggedy Anns
and Raggedy Andys by Knickerbocker, 15
in. (38 cm) and 18 in. (46 cm). Note the
robin's egg blue trousers and hat on the
Andy on the left, a departure from the
usual navy. The larger Andy has smaller
eyelashes and brighter hair, 1950 to 1980.

Knickerbocker novelties include two sizes of Raggedy Andy puppets and one of Ann. Huggies, at the bootom left, may be separated, but are usually left with their loving arms entwined, 1970s.

Musical Raggedy Andy, 15 in. (38 cm) by Knickerbocker with a wind-up music box encased in his body, 1970.

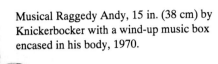

A group of Raggedy Ann and Raggedy Andy dolls. The large Andy in the back is from the 1960s and probably is home-made. Ann sitting next to him is of the same period by Knickerbocker, 40 in. (101 cm). A Georgene Ann sits on big Andy's lap, and the remaining are by Knickerbocker in sizes from a 6 in. (15 cm) hand puppet to a pair of 20 in. (51 cm) dolls, 1960 to 1970s.

The reverse side of a miniature box containing Knickerbocker dolls, 1970s.
Candy Brainard collection

The Camel with the Wrinkled Knees by Knickerbocker, mint in box, 1977; B M C Inc. *Candy Brainard collection*

The Camel with the Wrinkled Knees, 15 in. (38 cm) made by Knickerbocker of velour with a felt harness, © 1977.

Raggedy Ann and Raggedy Andy, 30 in. (76 cm) by Knickerbocker. This is a nice pair of originally clothed dolls in fine condition, 1970s.

Hand-made Raggedy Andy, 24 in. (61 cm) of cotton with machine embroidered features, yarn hair, cotton and corduroy clothes. Hand-made Raggedy Andy, 19 in. (48 cm) in cotton muslin with machine embroidered features, yarn hair, cotton and ticking clothes. Both date from post-1970.

Raggedy Ann and Raggedy Andy, 16 in.
(41 cm) by Knickerbocker. Andy has a
replaced tie and Ann is missing her apron
and pantaloons, 1970s.

Hand-made Raggedy Ann, 20 in. (51 cm)
muslin body with embroidered features,
bright yarn hair, nicely made cotton blend
clothing, circa 1988.

Black Raggedy Ann and Raggedy Andy,
33 in. (84 cm). Home-made dolls in brown
cotton/polyester with black yarn hair,
painted faces, traditional and well made
clothes; a charming pair, 1980s.

Raggedy Anns made by doll artist Carol Furgeson of painted cloth with canvas wigs, 1990s. *Candy Brainard collection*

Raggedy Ann, 16 in. (41 cm) made by Hasbro for Christmas of 1989. *Candy Brainard collection*

Raggedy Anns, 24 in. (61 cm) hand-made by a home seamstress of muslin with cotton clothes, applique and embroidered faces, roll-around eyes, yarn hair, circa 1970.

Related Playthings

The list of related objects starring not only Raggedy Ann and Andy, but all the characters that appear in the book, is seemingly endless. I suspect if it were possible to amass every item manufactured, a catalogue of immense proportions would be necessary. I have attempted to show an interesting cross section, but this effort cannot be considered completely definitine.

Raggedy Ann and Raggedy Andy paper dolls by Whitman Co.,uncut, 1935. *Candy Brainard collection*

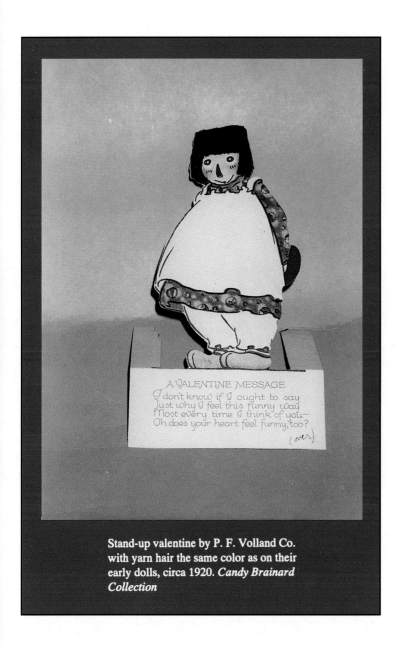

A VALENTINE MESSAGE
I don't know if I ought to say
Just why I feel this funny way
Most every time I think of you~
Oh does your heart feel funny, too?

(over)

Stand-up valentine by P. F. Volland Co. with yarn hair the same color as on their early dolls, circa 1920. *Candy Brainard Collection*

The companies producing various articles are legion. In many instances the book publishers distributed mementos and toys, as well. Bobbs-Merrill who began publishing the volumes in 1960 hosted a great variety. Their name may be found on high chairs, records, tea sets, watering cans, pillow kits, purses, kaleidoscopes, sew-ons, ventriloquist dummies and other fancies too numerous to itemize.

Wooden blocks made by Halsam, 1930s; six characters on each block and 12 blocks in each box.

The McMillan Company, as well as Hattie Carnegie, (best known perhaps as a milliner,) issued jewelry and silver Christmas ornaments. Among the outfits printing puzzles, games and paper dolls are Madman Quality, Saalfield, Milton Bradley and Whitman. Halsam made wooden blocks in various sizes; Hallmark and RCA labeled records; and McCalls printed patterns for costumes to fit young and old alike. I envision many party goers arriving as Raggedy Ann.

Raggedy Andy paper doll, 7 in. (18 cm); a cut-out version of Raggedy Andy with six articles of clothing and two hats, circa 1935.

The earlier china pieces made by Crooksville as well as Taylor, Smith and Taylor led the way to less breakable plastic by organizations such as Banner. Foreign companies like Janex of China presented a talking bank while Japan fashioned a ceramic nodder. Three dimentional "Puffy," prints typical of 1940s artwork saw the Artograph Co. making their version of the dynamic duo.

Doll artist Wendy Lawton, licensed by McMillan, charmed the collecting world with a bisque Marcella holding Ann, while The Ideal Company, known as an established doll maker, came out with a porcelain figure.

Children have always been able to indulge in their fantasy world with not only the dolls but the many playthings available. Of course the products are still being made for tots, but the adult collector is avid in their pursuit of all the wonderful dolls and memorabilia that had its genesis in the confines of a dusty garret.

Raggedy Ann paper doll, 7 in. (18 cm); cut-out figure with six outfits and two hats; a charming example of circa 1935 vintage.

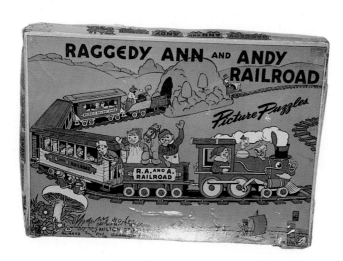

Raggedy Ann and Andy Railroad Picture Puzzles, 18 in. (46 cm) by Milton Bradley, 1940. Box contains six puzzles that form a train when combined. Riding in the cars are the main dolls plus other characters from the books. *Candy Brainard collection*

Raggedy Ann and Raggedy Andy pictured
on a creamware bowl made by Taylor,
Smith and Taylor, circa 1940.

Raggedy Ann and a soldier's face pictured
on a creamware bowl by Crooksville,
1940s.

Three pieces of a set decorated with
Raggedy Ann story characters, a plate, a
bowl and a divided dish manufactured by
Crooksville, circa 1940. *Candy Brainard
collection*

One of the train puzzles put together, 18 in. (46 cm). *Candy Brainard collection*

Raggedy Ann and Andy Paper Dolls and Clothes by Whitman Co., 1966. This set was designed for young children who could "press out" the clothes rather than cut them out. Raggedy Ann Color and Read book by Whitman Co, 1966 designed as a learning book for young children.

Raggedy Ann Tea Set of tin and plastic dinnerware and utensils by Banner, dated 1959, mint in box. *Candy Brainard collection*

Raggedy Ann game by Milton Bradley Company, 1954.

Raggedy Ann Push Button Marionette, 11
in. (28 cm) by Knickerbocker, shown with
original box, patent no. 3178852, circa
1970. *Candy Brainard collection*

Raggedy Ann Play Iron, 6 in. (15 cm),
(non electric) metal with plastic handle and
paper label made by Bobbs Merrill

45 RPM read along story record with a
pop- up picture inside the album by Bobbs
Merril, a Hallmark creation, 1974.

Glass ball Christmas ornaments featuring
Raggedy Ann and Raggedy Andy with
other animals enjoying winter activities;
issued by Bobbs Merrill in 1973. Judith
Armitstead collection

Glass ball Christmas ornaments featuring
Raggedy Ann issued one a year by
Schmid. *Judith Armitstead collection*

Goldtone Raggedy Ann figural pendant
with a heart on a chain which makes the
arms and legs move when pulled in the
manner of a jumping jack, 3 in. (8 cm)
including heart, suspended from a chain as
a necklace, by Hattie Carnegie, circa 1975.

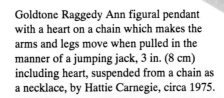

Set of six glass ball Christmas ornaments
featuring Raggedy Ann made by Corning
for Bobbs Merrill in 1974. *Judith
Armitstead collection*

Sewing pattern for Raggedy Ann and
Andy costumes by McCall's (in sizes for
children and adults), BMC Inc., 1978.
Candy Brainard collection

Raggedy Ann and Andy dolls, 16 in. (41 cm) with porcelain faces and hands by Ideal Corporation, © 1978. *Candy Brainard collection*

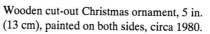

Wooden cut-out Christmas ornament, 5 in. (13 cm), painted on both sides, circa 1980.

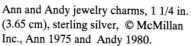

Ann and Andy jewelry charms, 1 1/4 in. (3.65 cm), sterling silver, © McMillan Inc., Ann 1975 and Andy 1980.

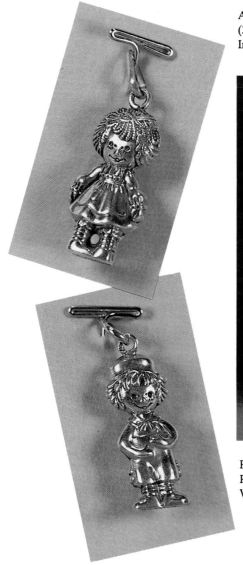

PUT DOLLS IN THIS HANDY CARRY-POCKET

Paper doll book, open page showing uncut Raggedy Ann figure published by Whitman, 1979.

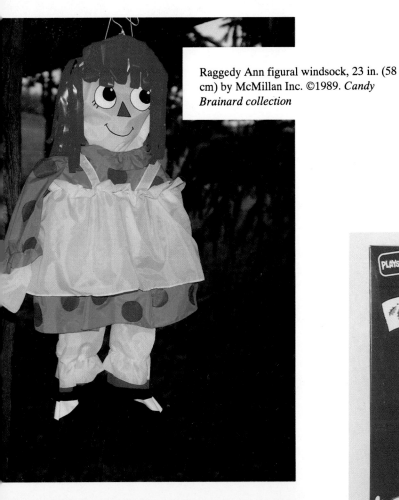

Raggedy Ann figural windsock, 23 in. (58 cm) by McMillan Inc. ©1989. *Candy Brainard collection*

Ann and Andy; 12 in; boxed set for Christmas 1990; Playschool, a division of Hasbro. *Bonnie and Larry Vaughan Collection*

Raggedy Ann and Andy decorated plate, 7 1/2 in. (19 cm) with a snow scene and assorted dolls, toy animals and E.T., souvenir issue, marked on back: "A Festival of Lights/ 1984/ a limited edition of 500 / " Raggedy Ann, Andy & Friends"/ Niagara Falls, N.Y." The Festival of Lights in Niagara Falls, N. Y. occurs annually in December when colored lights illuminate the falls. It is a scene of great beauty which attracts many people.

Chapter Three
The Golliwogg

Florence K. Upton and the Golliwogg

Webster's Dictionary describes "spinster" as an unmarried woman of gentle family and "lovelorn" as being bereft of love or a lover. The same source characterizes "psychic" as lying outside the sphere of physical science and a "painter" as an artist who paints. And so we have four words--spinster, lovelorn, psychic and painter. They are all descriptive of Florence K. Upton, but what a travesty it would be if this were her only epitaph. In fact her tombstone is inscribed "Creator Of The Golliwogg." Yet certainly this talented and complex woman was much more than that.

Florence was born on the 22nd day of February in the year 1873. Her English parents, Bertha and Thomas Harborough Upton, had emigrated to the United States from Hampstead, a fashionable area near London. It was on a journey back to this family homestead, to visit her grandmother, that Florence received a Blackamoor rag doll as a plaything. Fortunately, when it was discovered that the child had left it behind, her grandmother placed it in a trunk for safe keeping. Because her aunt resurrected it, years later, most sources assume the doll belonged to this relative. However, Florence's principal biographer, Edith Lyttleton, unequivocally states the original owner was Florence herself. Since Lyttleton was a personal friend, I must assume that her version is the correct one.

Florence and her three siblings enjoyed a normal and happy family environment. Their lifestyle was perhaps more interesting than average since the arts and travel played a role. Her father was an amateur painter who probably wielded his brush on Sunday outings to the park. Her mother was gifted with a pleasing singing voice and one can envision her exalting in a church choir. Bertha possessed a facility for words as well, especially rhymes, and this talent would come to the forefront in later years. Unfortunately, Thomas Upton succumbed in 1889, leaving his wife with four children, the eldest of whom was eighteen. The family struggled through grief and finally decided in 1893 to return to Hampstead to seek comfort in the bosom of their family.

Bertha Upton always had a desire to try her hand at writing for publication, and since Florence had inherited her father's gift of drawing, she suggested they collaborate. It was at this stage that the Black doll was revived and, as her daughter already had the wooden Dutch dolls to use as models, the characters were agreed upon. Fantasy took flight, for a book designed for children piqued their interest the most. Naming the black figure "golliwogg" certainly appears to have been Florence's

The Original Gilliwogg and dutch dolls that belonged to Florence K. Upton. They are presently on loan to the Bethnal Green Museum of Childhood in London. *Photograph courtesy of The Victoria and Albert Museum in South Kensington, London.*

A lovely square in the Chelsea section of London where Florence Upton had her studio. This beautiful neighborhood was home to many creative people. It is gratifying to tread the very streets where Florence Upton presumably walked as well.

Hand painted by Joan Allen who worked for Clarice Cliff in the 1930s and 1940s. She painted at home using any plate she could find and then had them fired at the factory.

inspiration, yet one expects the genesis to have had roots in some source other than the imagination. It has been suggested that the dark skinned natives working with British soldiers in occupied Egypt played a part. They wore arm bands initialed W.O.G.S. standing for "Working On Government Services." Florence ended the name with two "g"s but future works starring this creature often leave one "g" off and, in addition, it is often called a shortened Golly (or Golli.)

Using the Golliwogg and the wooden dolls as representatives, Florence finished thirty-one colored paintings and her mother completed corresponding verses. The finished manuscript was titled *The Adventures of two Dutch Dolls*. The hard task then ensued to find a publisher willing to take a risk; every door seemed to close upon her. No one seemed to particularly care for the pictures until Mr. Allen of Longman's Green & Co. realized they might hold a fascination for children.

The volume was released in 1895 to wide critical acclaim, and the rest, so the saying goes, is history. Although it was the wooden dolls that were featured in the title, it was the Golliwogg to whom children were attracted. Future works included them, but they never again appeared on the cover by name. By the publication day, Bertha had returned to the United States where she remained for the rest of her life. It was fortunate for mother and daughter to be so attuned for they were able to continue a long distance partnership with apparent ease. For the following fourteen years, Florence painted for the books and Bertha continued to send the verses.

Florence did not copyright her creation and so everyone was free to capitalize on her creative genius. The first book prompted the Golliwogg's likeness to be customized in doll form. Shop windows were full of them -- most hand-made and sporting seal skin hair. They soon became the most popular doll of their time, and emporiums selling them (along with a myriad of related items) realized thousands and thousands of pounds. It is safe to assume that the Upton's percentage was not as high, but they did continue with the saga and Florence was assured of a liveable income and a life-style suited to the period. In a letter from Paris dated April 19, 1902, she wrote that the Golliwogg was going to be dramatized at the Garrick Theatre in London and she was collaborating on the script. The final book made its appearance in 1909, and although Florence went on to other projects, it was not the end of the Golliwogg.

Purple pansies in a Chelsea, London windowbox that eerily seem to possess Golliwog faces.

The Adventures of two Dutch Dolls, the first book by Florence K. Upton, with verses by her mother Bertha; published by Longmans, Green and Company, London, 1895.

The storm clouds of war darkened Europe in the second decade of the twentieth century, and Florence, along with patriotic Britons, made her contribution to the war effort. On March 12, 1917 at 10:30 in the morning, she gathered all her personal momentoes together and proceeded by taxi to Christie's auction house. Ensconced beside her on the seat was a glass case containing the original Dutch dolls, the Golliwogg and 350 drawings. The artwork embraced fifty-six in frames and the balance in ten portfolios, all to be donated. She was hopeful that the lot might do well since they were catalogued to be sold directly after Queen Alexandra's gift to the Red Cross. The successful bid was ultimately made by Miss Faith Moore for nearly 500 pounds. She, in turn, donated the dolls to *Chequers* in Buckinghamshire, an estate that had been donated to the nation by Lord Lee of Fareham to be used as a country house for the Prime Minister. The dolls, still in their glass case, had found a permanent home. The paintings had been divided between the London Museum and the London Library where everyone could enjoy them.

On the fifth day of April in 1917, Florence met her friend, Lady Dawkins, at her residence in Chesham Place, for a meeting with Mr. Arthur Stanley and Sir Robert Hudson. The two gentlemen informed Florence that her most generous auction gift enabled the Red Cross to fully equip an ambulance. The vehicle was christened "Golliwogg" in large letters emblazoned on its side. Bertha Upton had been deceased for five years at this time so she never knew of this noble gesture.

When Florence ceased doing the illustrations for the popular children's books, she turned to a new career at her Chelsea Studio. This included primarily portraiture, painted both at this atelier and on her visits to America. The "Blue Room" was exhibited in the 1914 Salon at the Royal Academy, attesting to her great talent, since most artists aspire to be shown at this prestigious establishment. Her portrait of Viscount Milne in 1918 was presented to Balliol College by Lady Dawkins. Among her works are "Mrs. Ziegler and Kathleen" commissioned in 1913, and a 1924 study of Mr. Stanley Field painted in Chicago.

Although her professional life was full of acknowledged accomplishments, her private life fell far short of her hopes and dreams. Florence's friend, Edith Lyttleton, describes her existence as fraught with depression and unrealized contentment. She was constantly unhappy and distressed, yearning for companionship and love. A life-long commitment continued to allude her, but perhaps *because* of this loneliness and introspection, she experienced psychic phenomena. Because this was a recurring feeling, she began to research and work at it with wholehearted zeal. Whenever Florence was faced with an interest or task, she proceeded tenaciously.

The end of her life was full of illness and great suffering, and although she was denied the husband she desired to see her through a crisis, she was fortunate to have a friend who remained at her side. Florence implored this friend to tell her when death seemed imminent and this final request was granted. In spite of her psychic awareness, she refused to give this credence and closed her eyes for the last time at the age of 49, not realizing that life was indeed at an end.

The Golliwogg's Adventures

The first book embracing the Golliwogg and the Dutch dolls, by Florence and Bertha Upton, set the tone for the volumes that followed. The format, published by Longmans, Green and Co, is oblong in 4 to quarto with a binding of glazed, pictorially printed paper covered boards and is further enhanced by a cloth spine. All thirteen have 64 pages of text and illustrations and are printed by the lithography method.

The Golliwogg's Bicycle Club by Florence K. Upton and verses by Bertha Upton, Longmans, Green & Co., London, New York & Bombay, 1903. Dolls and Golli travel around the world.

1. *The Adventures of Two Dutch Dolls.* 1895
2. *The Golliwogg's Bicycle Club.* 1896
3. *The Golliwogg at the Sea-Side.* 1898
4. *The Golliwogg In War!* 1899
5. *The Golliwogg's Polar Adventures.* 1900
6. *The Golliwogg's Auto-Go-Cart.* 1901
7. *The Golliwogg's Air-Ship.* 1902
8. *The Golliwogg's Circus.* 1903
9. *The Golliwogg In Holland.* 1904
10. *The Golliwogg's Fox Hunt.* 1905
11. *The Golliwogg's Desert Island.* 1906
12. *The Golliwogg's Christmas.* 1907
13. *The Golliwoggs in the African Jungle.* 1909

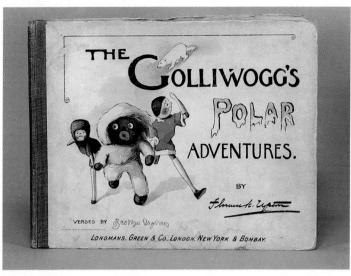

Collecting and acquiring the complete set is a task that normally involves several years of searching. Even with the aid of old book dealers it is not a hobby than can be completed in record time. *The Golliwogg's Christmas* is the most elusive of all and is usually the last volume to be found.

When Florence and Bertha no longer penned the Golliwogg stories, other authors used the character to their own advantage. The intermingling of the Golli with the Teddy bear was a common occurence since, while the black figure was best known in Great Britain, the bruin was popular internationally. One of the first publications to appear, *The Teddy Bearoplane,* is as avidly sought by arctophiles as by the Golli aficionado. Fay Inchfawn wrote *The Golliwogg News* in 1914 and Murray Fisher included not only Golli, but the Dutch doll in his 1919 opus *The Famousness of Nancy the Dutch Doll.*

The Golliwogg's Polar Adventures by Florence K. Upton and verses by Bertha Upton, Longmans, Green and Company, London, 1900.

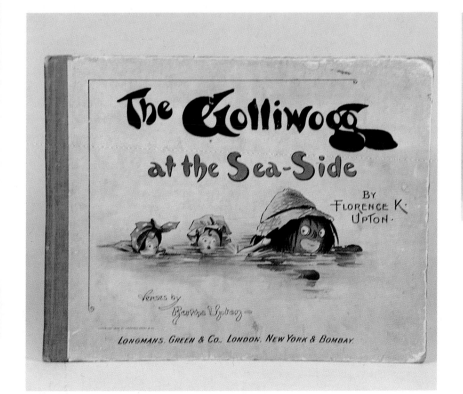

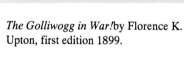

The Golliwogg in War! by Florence K. Upton, first edition 1899.

The Golliwogg at the Seaside by Florence K. Upton, first edition 1898.

The Golliwogg's Auto-Go-Cart by
Florence K. Upton, © 1901.

The Golliwogg's Circus by Florence K.
Upton and verses by Bertha Upton,
Longmans, Green & Co., London, New
York & Bombay, © 1903, printed by
Niagara Lith. Co., Buffalo, N.Y. The dolls
and Golli put on a circus, first edition.

The Golliwogg's Air-Ship by Florence K.
Upton and verses by Bertha Upton,
Longmans, Green & Co., London, New
York & Bombay, © 1902. The wooden
dolls and Golli build and have adventures
in a hot air balloon, first edition.

The Golliwogg in Holland by Florence K.
Upton and verses by Bertha Upton, first
edition 1904.

The Golliwogg's Christmas by Florence K. Upton and verses by Bertha Upton, first edition 1907.

The Golliwogg's Desert Island by Florence K. Upton and verses by Bertha Upton, © 1906.

The Goliwogg's Fox-Hunt by Florence K. Upton and verses by Bertha Upton, © 1905.

The Vege-Men's Revenge by Florence K. Upton and verses by Bertha Upton, first edition 1897. This book is one that is not about Golliwogg although the size and format are the same. The paintings are beautifully rendered and imaginative but have a softer, more ethereal quality.

The Teddy Bearoplane by May Byron, illustrated by J. R. Sinclair, published by Hodder & Stoughton, printed in England by the Acme Tone Engraving and Printing Co., Watford, no date but advertised in *The Bookseller* in 1911.

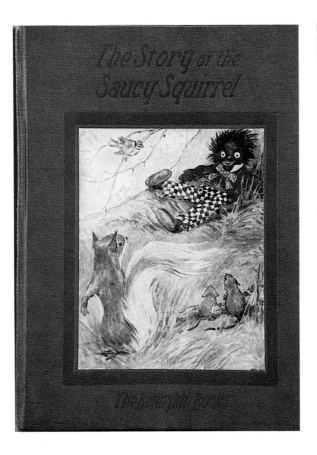

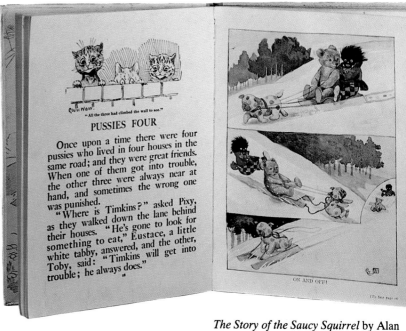

The Playtime Story Book published by Ward, Loch and Co. Limited, London and Melbourne, © 1910. This is an adventure story with children, Golliwogg, cats and dogs.

The Story of the Saucy Squirrel by Alan Wright, George W. Jacobs & Co. publishers, 1920. This story of a squirrel features Golliwogg on the cover.

Pussies and Puppies, published by Sam'l Gabriel Sons and Company, circa 1920. A wash fabric book, this features Golliwogg on the cover.

Cover of *The Chummy Book* with harlequin-dressed Golliwogg and a dressed teddy bear which appears to be from the 1920s.

Old Mister Bear Comes Home figural shape book, Whitman Publishing Co., Racine, Wisc. Six stories include Golliwogg, circa 1935.

Billie's Two Chums

On Christmas morning, Billie's first surprise as he looked at his stocking was to see two funny little faces looking at him. One was Teddy Bear and the other was Golly.

Perhaps you do not know what a golly is. It is a funny little black doll. It is blacker than a pickaninny, almost jet black with funny woolly hair, big white eyes, and a very funny look.

For Billie, Golly and Teddy Bear were the best of all his gifts. He called them twins because they both came on the same day.

Everyone called Billie a very quiet boy, but Golly and Teddy Bear knew better. Billie was rather noisy in his fun with them, and the three had a rollicking time.

One morning Mother said, "Aunt Mary and Cousin Jane are coming for a visit." Billie did not remember Aunt Mary or Cousin Jane, for they came from Kansas; but when he found out that Cousin Jane was six, just one year older than he, he was sure it was all going to be fun and was very happy.

Jane, at first, would have nothing to do with Golly, he was so queer and strange. She would play with Teddy Bear and as long as Billie did not have Golly about, she would play with him. But whenever Golly appeared, she would stop playing and hurry to her mother.

Billie did not know what to do. He did not want to leave Golly alone, but what could he do? Golly looked so sad and so funny, Billie almost wished Jane had never come to visit them.

One afternoon, Billie went to the grocery with his mother, and Jane was left alone. Mother and Billie were gone an hour; and when they returned, imagine Billie's surprise to see Jane playing with Golly and happy in doing it.

And then Jane explained. She had gone to the toy room to find Teddy Bear, had picked him up. Then as she turned to look, she saw that funny, sad look in Golly's face. All of a sudden she knew she would like Golly. When she picked Golly up too and started to play with both Teddy and Golly, Golly almost laughed aloud with happiness.

All through Jane's visit, Golly was never again left out of the children's play.

Color frontispiece from *Teddy Bear's Circus* including Golliwogg. This book by Constance Wickham and illustrated by A. E. Kennedy was published by Collins in London and Glasgow, © 1946, this a 1953 edition in hard cover with dust jacket. French editions by this author include *Le Cirque de Lours Teddy*, *Lours Teddy*, *Le petite Negre Bambo* and *Au Pays des Betes*.

The Teddy Bear Book in linenette soft cover, all color illustrations featuring a teddy bear and Golliwogg; published by Whitman Co., 1940, including 14 pages with Golliwogg on 11 of them.

Teddy's Tea Party, 10 in. (25 cm) in paper cover with illustrations by Sylvia I. Venus and marked "Nursery series No. 4", Monomark B. C. M. R N I K Z, the story of a party from invitation to event, circa 1945.

Magic Island by Clifford Webb, published by Frederich Warne & Co. Ltd., London and New York, © 1956, the story of a Golli who turns into a boy and has adventures with his owners.

Toy Town Day by Day by Frances Woof, P. M. Productions, Ltd., London, circa 1954, 12 pages including covers. The story relates the activities of Toylands inhabitants during each day of the week. The main characters are Golly and Teddy bear twins. *Courtesy of Doris Frohnsdorff.*

Maxie and the Gollybear by Alys Myers, illustrated by Maxwell, published by Birn Brothers Ltd., London, circa 1950. This is the story of a headless teddy bear that got the head of a Golliwogg who had no body.

Golly Runs Away, paper format published by Birn Bros. Ltd., London, printed in England, circa 1950. In this story Golly leaves the nursery and finds adventures.

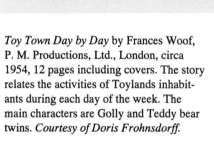

Georgie Golliwog by Frances Woof, London, circa 1954, folio of 20 pages, this being the original drawing of the cover. The story is about the Golliwog's acts of heroism and kindness: at Christmas time he saves the golden haired angel and they get married and ride off in a convertible sports car. *Courtesy of Doris Frohnsdorff*

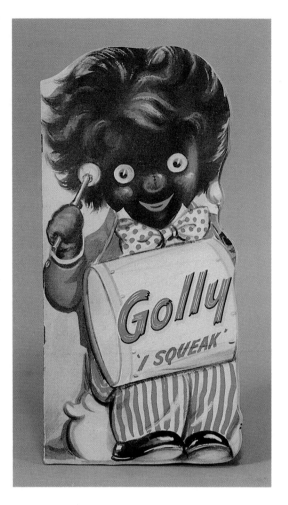

The following decade saw the continuance of this creature's popularity celebrated in many books issued in England. A few American firms, such as Whitman and Sam'l Gabriel, included Golli in their publications as well. Further proof of his appeal can be attested to the fact that his likeness might appear on a cover, yet the inside would carry nary a trace. Obviously Golli was used to merely attract. During the 1930 s and 1940 s, he continued to be featured, but it was during the 50 s that a new surge of interest prompted book after book. Among them is the "Noddy" series in which a wooden elfin-like doll is joined by a Golli and often a bear as they seek adventure. Fanciful ideas appeared such as the "I Squeak" novelty. This figural format has an internal squeaker imbedded in the cover to afford additional amusement.

It is apparent that many lovers of the Golliwogg start out by collecting the Upton books and find their appetite so whetted that everything that carries Golli's name or picture is amassed as well.

Golly 'I Squeak', 10 in. (25 cm), figural shape, circa 1950, English. This story of Golly in Toyland includes a squeaker inbedded in the back cover.

Noddy and his Car small format book by Enid Blyton with pictures by Beek, published by Sampson, Low, Marston & Co. Ltd. and Dennis Dobson Ltd., London, © 1951. This is one of a series featuring the adventures of a wooden man and a Golliwogg. The cookie tin contained Huntley and Palmer Iced Biscuits for Children, "Noddy" rights © 1971.

Teddy, Golly, and Bunny, 10 in. (25 cm) hard cover book by Constance Wickham, illustrated by Kennedy, published by Collins, London and Glasgow. This charming format has cartoons, numbers, and adventures; circa 1950.

In *Golly Runs Away*, once again it is evident that Golliwogg and teddy bears are intertwined.

Inside *Golly 'I Squeak'*, Golli squeezes by the teddy bear.

" that's what I'll do. I'll run away ! "

So that night he carefully put Mrs. Noah back on the Noah's Ark, and he crept past a jig-saw puzzle, and he slipped behind Susanna, the doll who said " Mama " when you turned her upside down, and he squee-ee-eezed past the teddy bear,

He waited until it was late and the moon was shining, then he pushed open the door of the cupboard and softly crept out.

There was no sound but the tick-tock of the old grandfather clock and the rustle of a mouse somewhere.

Golly found out. He slid of the garden He felt qu had no idea ing till he car were open he

Rufty Tufty Makes a House in hard cover with dust jacket by Ruth Ainsworth, published by Heineman, London, 1965 with small black and white illustrations. This story of Mr. and Mrs. Golly is one of seven titles in a series.

RUFTY TUFTY
MAKES A HOUSE

HORSESHOE HOUSE

RUTH AINSWORTH

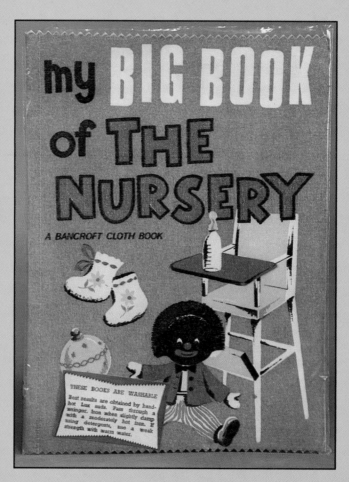

My Big Book of the Nursery cloth book
that is washable and still in its original
plastic wrapper with washing instructions,
published by Banroft & Co. Ltd., London,
© 1967.

Golliwogg Dolls

The earliest known commercially made Golliwoggs were manufactured by the Margarete Steiff Company in Giengen, Germany. This doll was fully articulated and came in sizes of 11, 13, 17, 20, 24, 32, and 39 inches. In the manner of most of this firm's dolls, the clothes form the body and therefore are not removable. His outfit consists of a white vest, a red necktie and trousers, and a blue jacket. Golli has shoe button eyes backed by red and white felt, a red felt smiling mouth that reveals white teeth, a mohair wig, and he stands sturdily in black leather boots. Although he was in production from 1908 until 1916 or 1917, he does not surface with any frequency. In 1908, a limited number of a snap-apart version was introduced, and from 1909 until 1920, a roly-poly entered the field.

Schuco, a German organization known for inventive and superlative mechanicals, advertised a Black doll in their 1924 catalog. Their version of Golli was traditionally executed, but had the addition of a "voice." The same periodical featured a Golliwogg jack-in-the-box as well.

In the first few decades of the twentieth century, the Sonneberg/Thuringia area of Germany was recognized as the toy capitol of the world. Between the two World Wars, three Hermann brothers (Artur, Bernhard, and Max) each had their own companies. Max began the enterprise known as Hermann Spielwaren Gmb. H in Coburg, and it is still in business making teddy bears as their primary toy. Another firm, Leven, made a great variety of children's playthings, including a Golliwogg. Several catalogs, from 1925 until 1931, pictured Golli in three or four sizes and with slight changes in dress as the years progressed. The Founder of Leven had no children so eventually sold the company to Mr. Fred Engel. One of Mr. Engel's daughters married Max Hermann's son Rolf, and *their* daughter, Dona-Margot, became sole heir to the Leven Company. Thus. we find the connection between the two firms. In 1992, Hermann re-issued the Leven Golliwogg in two sizes, and with attached tags that relate the interesting and historical story.

In England, birthplace of the movement, we find, for the most part, the dolls being hand-made on an individual basis during the earliest years. Some of these characters are very well executed, but even if the creator is not a supreme seamstress, the Golli most often has a charm likened to folk art. Imagination ran high and now collectors can assemble superlative examples of one-of-a-kind Golliwoggs.

In 1923, Dean's (first located in London and ultimately finding a home in Wales) introduced *Wooly Wally*. The catalog described him as "brightly dressed, strongly made, the wild wig is like the tame smile - it won't come off." Complete with spats, he also was available in a model sitting on a fold-up scooter. Since that time, the Golliwogg has appeared with fair regularity in the Dean's line.

Another English firm, Chad Valley, launched a version in 1929 placing their logo button on the back under the clothes. Merrythought (located in Shropshire) produced a Golliwogg as their first venture in doll making. This doll, born in 1932, came in three sizes of 16, 18 and 22 inches. By 1934, a slumbering Golli was added, and in 1935 the traditional doll was made in six sizes. Over the ensuing years, variations appeared including a 1949-1955 Jollywog (a 1964 all-jointed doll) and a long-legged creature named Lanky Joe. Merrythought has continued to offer this favorite toy right up to the present.

Golliwogg collectors have increased in number and we can be assured production will continue to satisfy their growing interest.

These wonderful early Golliwogg dolls, 14 in. (36 cm), are a rare pair that were in store windows during the publication of Florence Upton's books. Both the male and female are made of wool with cotton clothes, the eyes are buttons, and the nose is three dimensional rather than suggested. Although the hair on this pair is white fur (probably rabbit), it was more commonly found with black sealskin.

Golliwogg girl, 2 in. (5 cm), a hand-made miniature girl Golliwogg with a black cotton body, embroidered curly hair, embroidered features, detailed pink silk dress, circa 1915.

Golliwogg dolls, 10 in. (25 cm), which are wonderful early examples of the sort found in stores around 1910-1920 with molded fabric and painted faces, sealskin hair, cotton bodies stuffed with excelsior, and felt clothes; they retain the original price tags of 9 pence.

Charming Golliwogg doll, 15 in. (38 cm), circa 1920 with wooden eyes, needle stitched nose, embroidered mouth, sealskin hair, unusual embroidery to simulate fingers and toes in the manner of teddy bear claws, extremely long legs and colorful clothes, made in England.

World War I Golliwogg, 10 in. hand-made doll with embroidered features, pearl eyes, sealskin hair, and a non-removable soldiers uniform with leather trim. *Maria Bluni collection*

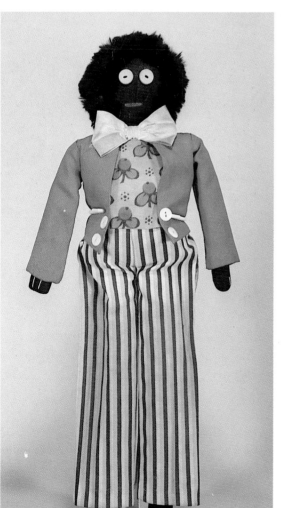

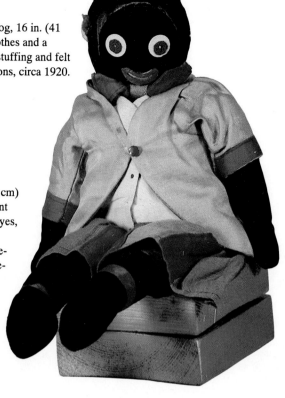

Hand-made English Golliwog, 16 in. (41 cm) with colorful sateen clothes and a velvet body over excelsior stuffing and felt eyes backed with bone buttons, circa 1920.

Hand-made Golliwogg doll, 11 in. (28 cm) with stitched teeth and a mouth different from the usual solid lips, shoe button eyes, and sealskin hair. This doll is rather crudely executed but of value never-the-less and appears to have been made pre-1930, English.

Handmade Golliwogg dolls, 5 in. (13 cm), with sealskin hair, made in England, pre-1920.

Golliwogg, 15 in. (38 cm), with sateen fabric, felt mouth, collar and cuffs, bead eyes, and sealskin hair, English, pre-1930.

Golliwogg, 19 in. (48 cm) with black
cotton body, sewn-on felt features,
sealskin hair, and cotton clothes with
brocade jacket lapels, English, circa 1925.

Hand-made Golliwogg, 12 1/2 in. made
with ribbed fabric for face and hands,
curled yarn hair, felt clothes and features,
nicely detailed especially the shoes, circa
1935.

Golliwogg, 18 in. (46 cm), hand-made in
England, circa 1930.

Golliwogg, 15 in. (38 cm) in red, white
and blue silky plush, black plush hair and a
celluloid face with googly eyes that move
easily, English, circa 1935.

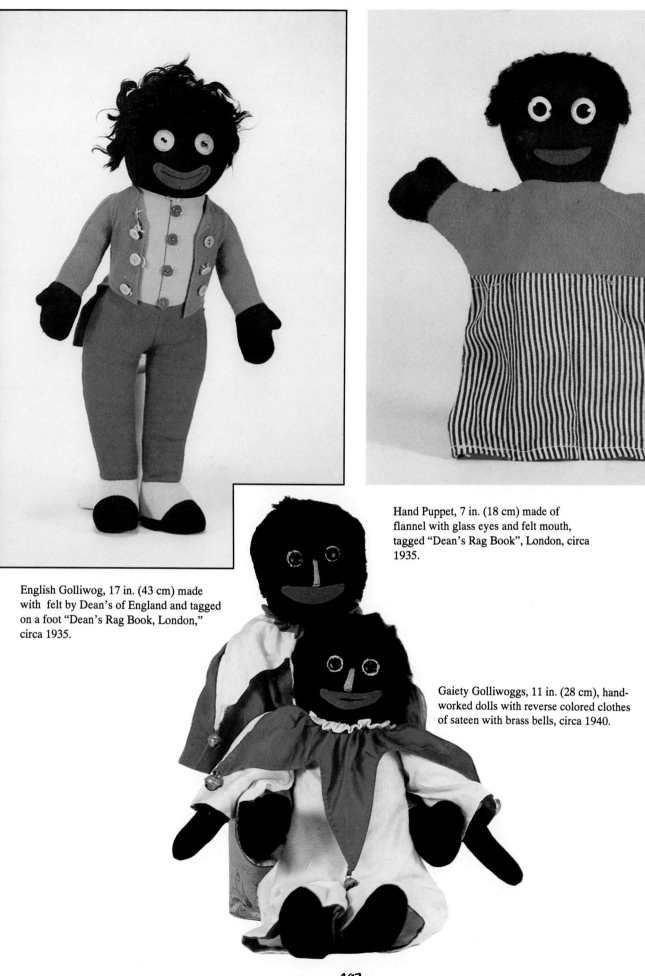

Hand Puppet, 7 in. (18 cm) made of flannel with glass eyes and felt mouth, tagged "Dean's Rag Book", London, circa 1935.

English Golliwog, 17 in. (43 cm) made with felt by Dean's of England and tagged on a foot "Dean's Rag Book, London," circa 1935.

Gaiety Golliwoggs, 11 in. (28 cm), hand-worked dolls with reverse colored clothes of sateen with brass bells, circa 1940.

Hand-made Golliwogg, 24 in. (61 cm) in black cotton with felt eyes and mouth, curly yarn hair, nicely detailed cotton clothes circa 1950.

Knit Golliwogg, 13 in. made extremely well by a home knitter, 1950-1960s. Knit coat hanger, 12 in. wooden hanger covered with a Golli's head as decoration, home-made, 1950s-60s. *Maria Bluni collection*

Above Right: Golliwogg, 9 in. (23 cm), all cotton hand made doll, circa 1950.

Golliwogg, 15 in. (38 cm) of cotton and felt with sewn-on features and plush hair, English, circa 1950.

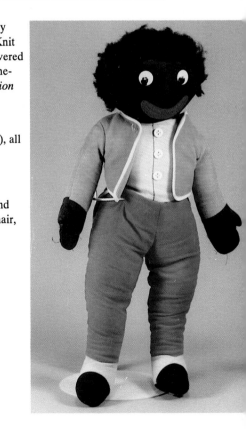

Merrythought Golliwogg, 20 in. (51 cm), with cotton and felt clothes in a typical look of the 1950s era.

Golliwogg, 13 in. (33 cm), hand-knit doll typical of the 1950s.

Knitted Golliwogg, 10 in. (25 cm). The 1950s era saw many homemakers knitting Gollis for their children; this nice example is in fine condition with yarn features and side-glancing eyes.

Golliwog, 19 in. (48 cm) made in England by Merrythought Company of Ironbridge, Shropshire, 1950s.

Hand-knit Golliwoggs, l9 in. (48 cm) and 18 in. (46 cm), English, typical of those made in the 1950s.

A pair of knit Golliwogg twins, 11 in. (28 cm), with an odd shoe treatment but overall typical of 1950s home-made dolls.

Golliwogg, 12 in. (31 cm) made by Wendy Boston in a print featuring her name and several animals over foam filling, circa 1965.

English Golliwogg, 15 in. (38 cm) of felt with roll-around eyes. This appears to be a 1940-1950 production manufactured by Dean's of England.

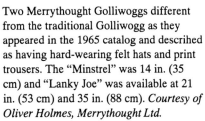

Two Merrythought Golliwoggs different from the traditional Golliwogg as they appeared in the 1965 catalog and described as having hard-wearing felt hats and print trousers. The "Minstrel" was 14 in. (35 cm) and "Lanky Joe" was available at 21 in. (53 cm) and 35 in. (88 cm). *Courtesy of Oliver Holmes, Merrythought Ltd.*

Left: Chad Valley/Chiltern Golliwogg, 16 in. (41 cm) with black cotton face and soles, white cotton hands, shirt and feet, striped cotton pants, felt features and jacket, plush hair, soft stuffing, circa 1970. A satin label on a side seam reads "Chad Valley/Chiltern/ Hygienic toys/Made in England." **Center**: Merrythought Golliwogg, 14 in. (36 cm) with black cotton face and foot soles, yellow cotton hands, feet, and shirt, striped cotton pants, felt mouth, nose and jacket, plastic googly eyes, plush hair, and soft stuffing, circa 1955, no marks. **Right**: Golliwog, 11 1/2 in. (29 cm), possibly made as Robertson's give-away premium with black cotton face, hands, and feet, yellow cotton shirt, red cotton pants, felt features and jacket, and soft stuffing, circa 1950-1960, no marks.

Golliwogg, 13 in. (33 cm) in printed fabric with plastic eyes and plush hair tagged "Dean's Childsplay Toys Ltd, England", circa 1960.

Golliwogg, 22 in. (56 cm) with velvet face, googly eyes, plastic mouth, corduroy and flannel clothes, pull voice box, made by Pedigree, Ireland, circa 1960.

All-felt Golliwogg, 12 in. (31 cm) with colorful clothes and top hat, English, probably home-sewn, circa 1960.

Golliwogg, 11 in. (28 cm) by Wendy Boston in a simple design with the recognizable face used by this designer, circa 1960, tagged "Wendy Boston/made in England."

Golliwogg, 30 in. (76 cm) of plush with felt mouth and plastic eyes, rhinestone bow tie, English, circa 1965.

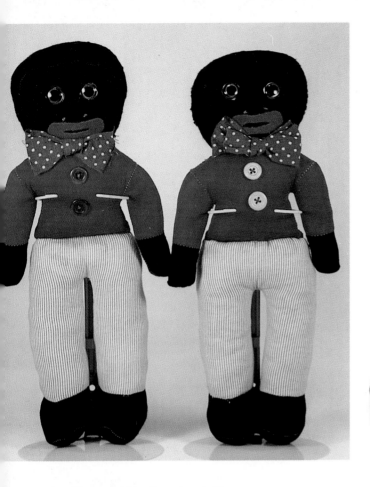

Twin Golliwoggs, 16 in. (41 cm) probably made in the 1960s in cotton with wooly hair; only their buttons are different.

Golliwogg, 25 in. (64 cm), cotton with felt pasted-on features, English, circa 1960.

Merrythought Golliwogg, 20 in. (51 cm) in velvet and velour with chimes in the body that ring as Golli is moved, circa 1965.

Two Golliwoggs, 13 in. (33 cm) and 14 in. (36 cm), both commercial dolls, English, circa 1960.

Dean's of England Golliwogg, 13 in., made
of printed fabric with removeable felt coat,
tagged in seam, circa 1960. Merrythought
Golliwogg, 14 in., made of velour with
glass googly eyes as was typical of this
company's charming examples, circa
1960.

English Golliwogg, 17 in. (43 cm) felt,
cotton and corduroy doll commercially
made, not tagged, circa 1960.

Pedigree Golliwogg, 15 in. (38 cm) made
of felt and cotton with pasted on features,
made in Ireland, circa 1960.

Wendy Boston Golliwogg, 20 in. made of
polyester fabric with felt coat, glued-on
features, and the designer's signature
eyebrows, circa 1960. English Golliwogg,
18 in. of cotton printed fabric, painted
features, plush hair, manufacturer
unknown, circa 1960.

Three Chad Valley Golliwoggs, 13 in., 15 in., and 11 in., made of cotton with usual striped pants. The 13-inch example has glued-on felt features while the other two have painted eyes and mouth; all have plush hair and are typical of 1950s and 1960s production.

Merrythought Golliwogg, 15 in. (38 cm), all-felt doll with plastic eyes, circa 1960.

English Golliwogg, 13 in. made of red, white and blue plush with felt eyes and mouth, circa 1970.

Golliwogg with plastic guitar, 19 in. (48 cm), made by Wendy Boston with polyester clothes, English, circa 1970.

Knit Golliwogg, 8 in. (20 cm). This colorful hand knit toy style was popular in England circa 1970-1980.

Pedigree Golliwogg, 24 in. (61 cm), made of felt and corduroy with painted vinyl eyes and large plastic mouth and tagged "Pedigree Ireland", circa 1970. Plush Golliwogg, 19 in. (48 cm), English example of 1970s or 1980s production with a plush body and polyester head.

Hand-made Golliwogg, 48 in. (112 cm).
This large doll is all velvet with roll-
around eyes, 1980s.

Contemporary Golliwoggs, 18 in. (46 cm)
and 16 in. (41 cm), 1990s production from
the English firm of Dean's located in
Wales. Distributed in the United States by
Hobby House Press. It is made of velvet
and cotton with roll-around eyes.

Golliwogg, 18 in. (46 cm) made with plush
and synthetic fabrics and roll-around eyes,
British, circa 1975.

Merrythought Golliwogg, 20 in. (51 cm), with a black velour face, hands and slippers and white velour feet, plush hair, plastic eyes and nose, a glued-on mouth, cotton non-removeable clothes, and soft stuffing, 1986. A cloth tag on back seam and a tag on the left sole read "Merrythought Ironbridge Shrops, Made in England."

Artist Golliwogg, 4 1/2 in. (5 cm). This wonderful detailed Golliwogg was created by America's premier Golli artist, Kathy Thomas, with leather face, gloves and shoes, a felt shirt, ultra-suede pants and jacket, sealskin hair, some painting and tiny beads add to the detail. It is signed under the coat tails and dated 1989, is one of a series and is highly sought by collectors.

Golliwogg replicas, l9 in. (39 cm) and 14 in. (36 cm), made of velour, felt and cotton by Hermann Spielwaren, these 1925 Leven Replicas were made in 1992. They are stamped on the feet and come with attached booklets telling the story of the Leven - Hermann connection.

Oh Golly!, 4 in., designed and made by canadian artist Trudy Yelland with velour face and hands, plush hair, felt jacket and features. This is Number 1 in a limited edition, 1993.

Golly, Gollis Everywhere!

Although the Golliwog doll ranks supreme among collectors, it is difficult not to be entranced with his likeness in all mediums. From the time the first book was published with such stunning success, his image has appeared on china, paper, advertising, and playthings of all kinds.

One can envision a small child sitting at the nursery tea table surrounded by bisque dolls and with a Golliwogg as the guest of honor. The table would be laden with hand painted or transfer-designed china all embellished with the black figure shown in a variety of activities. Many of the pieces are after Upton's work and copyrighted by her publisher. Other manufacturers had their own diverse interpretations. The majority of china was manufactured in Great Britain, but the occasional item bears the stamp of another nation. Although table settings are prevalent, china was utilized in other ways. Figurines, given as premiums by the Robertson Company, were joined in mid-century by two Royal Doulton charmers.

Bonnie Prince and his Christmas Golli, 13 1/2 in. bear and 7 in. Golliwogg designed and made by Dee Hockenberry. Golli has a faux leather face, mohair wig, and felt made-on clothes and features. He is fully jointed and one of a one-of-a-kind pair donated to The Toy And Miniature Museum auction in 1993 in Kansas City.

Robertson's---purveyors of marmalade, jams and other condiments, seems to be the fore-runner for using the Golli image as a logo. Golli emerges on advertising signs, labels, and of course on an enormous selection of premiums, thus making this enterprise and Golliwog almost synonymous. The design has remained fairly constant, except one can note the rounder head and centered eyeballs used prior to 1950. Inexpensive tin pinbacks can be found, but the enameled pins tend to be more collectible. A great array of musicians, sports figures and occupations have been made right up to the present day. At first, "golden Shred" (marmalade) appeared on the chest area of the pin, and eventually this was eliminated in favor of the organization's name being printed on the reverse. China bowls and plaster or china musicians are among the many articles introduced over the years.

Certainly the black fellow is most identified with jams, but other companies benefited by his likeness, too. He graced trade cards promoting a variety of products and enticed homemakers to use a certain wax (to name just a few.) During the jazz era when an abundance of imaginative items were in vogue, de Vigny of France came out with "le Golliwogg" parfum. The bottle featured a seal skin wigged head as the stopper and came in a satin lined presentation box.

In addition to the doll, other playthings featured his image where he sometimes just came into view in a minor way. One of the cleverest is the animated theater affording hours of fanciful activity. Simple objects such as clickers, sand pails and dancing toys were, and are, available as well as blocks. A ceramic bank with rollaround eyes as well as a bronze full-figured money box encouraged thrift.

Ephemera has always played an important part in the collecting arena. Post and greeting cards, paper dolls and wrapping paper, and even more exotic images such as the Steiff stamps and Raphael Tuck rockers can be counted. In the area of prints, it is interesting to see Golli teamed with other famous persona such as Teddy and Bonzo.

The list of Golliwogg-related momentoes is seemingly endless. It is possible to amass an enviable array by choosing just one medium or to collect, as most do, everything that features Florence Upton's legacy.

Bronze Golliwogg still bank, 6 in. (15 cm), with a money slot in the back. Evidently the bank also was made in painted cast

The Three Bears puzzle blocks is a charming set with a linnenette book in a box. The blocks show a variety of scenes including one of a children's nursery featuring a Golliwogg. It was printed in Bavaria, circa 1897, and marked "E N Trademark."

Pendulum clock, 7 in. (18 cm) plus pendulum and weight, the clock face is painted with a child and Golliwogg. The wooden works are weight-driven and when the pendulum swings, the eyes on the child move back and forth; Germany, circa 1900, no mark.

Puppet theatre in its original box, circa 1900 by Mathews & Co., Limited, Leicester, England. The stage folds flat and also becomes dimentional. The set includes a wire puppet manipulator and the puppets include a wooden doll, a Golliwogg, a trick dog riding a bear, a cat, a clown, and a china doll. All the puppet limbs are moveable, including the dog's head with a ruff. This wonderful and rare toy possibly was made for the French market, circa 1900.

Wooden Golliwogg pop-up game with lithographed paper showing dolls, Golliwogg and a teddy bear surrounding the bulls-eye. When an object hits the circle, a spring-loaded Golliwogg pops up from the back; German, circa 1900.

Ceramic cup and plate of child's size decorated with a design taken from Florence Upton's book *The Golliwogg's Polar Adventure*, 1900, no marks.

Ceramic plate, cup and saucer from a full service, the dessert plate is 6 in. (15 cm) in diameter. The decoration is hand painted with designs after Florence K. Upton's figures, finely detailed, circa 1905. English, stamped on the bottom "R.E.G./ A 25169."

Ceramic plate, 5 in. (13 cm) decorated with Forence Upton's figures, English, circa 1900.

Austrian bronze miniature figure, 1 1/4 in., of a Golliwogg and a wooden doll sitting on a park bench, circa 1900. *Bill Boyd collection*

Post card with Florence K Upton's illustration *"Golliwogg" Motoring*, produced by Raphael Tuck with permission of Longman's Green and Co, circa 1900. *Susan Brown Nicholson collection*

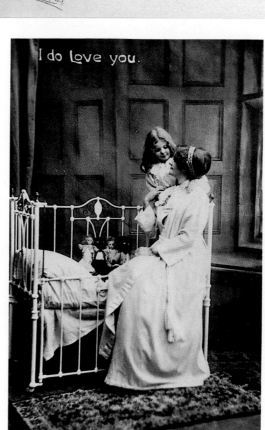

Trade post card showing children under a tree with their mother and Golliwogg to advertise using the London Underground system "for pleasure parties," this one is slightly larger than a regular post card, circa 1900. Birthday greeting post card with Mr. and Mrs. Golliwogg, English, circa 1904.

Photograph post card in sepia tone depicting a bedtime nursery scene with Golliwoggs and dolls in the crib, Davidson Brothers, London and New York, circa 1900.

Individual print from a Florence Upton book page, © 1899 by Longman, Green & Co.

Post card "Evening Prayers" with Florence Upton's storybook characters, circa 1900. Post card with Flornce K. Upton's illustation *"Golliwogg" & the Highwayman* printed by Raphael Tuck, circa 1900. *Susan Brown Nicholson collection*

Two Golliwogg folding greeting cards for the holiday season including Florence Upton's drawings with Bertha Upton's verses, ©1900 with permission of Longmans Green & Co.; printed by Raphael Tuck.

Golliwogg Christmas card, 4 1/4 in. (11 cm) small format fold-out with an illustration taken from the Florence Upton books, circa 1900, unmarked.

Post card with the illustration *The "Golliwogg" come to grief on the ice* from a Florence Upton book, reproduced by Permission of Messrs. Longman, Green & Co., circa 1900.

Golliwogg game of 46 cards in a box, each card having a different picture. Manufactured to his majesty by Thomas De La Rue and Co. Ltd. 110 Bunhill Row, London, after Florence Upton designs and with permission of Longman, Green & Co., circa 1900.

Figural lithograph card produced by Raphael Tuck, circa 1900. The child depicted holds a typical version of an early Golliwog. The card has a folding stand on the back.

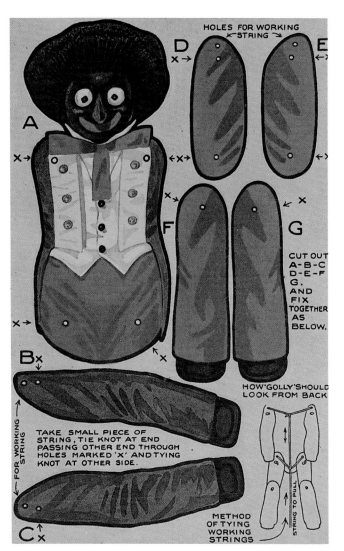

Rocking card "The Glad Golliwogg"
published by Raphael Tuck with the
following verse: "To jump this merry child
upon my knee," said Golliwogg, "is just
the fun for me! She used to seem afraid
because my hair is black as coals, but now
she doesn't care." circa 1905.

"Golywog" paper doll pantin and its
original envelope. When cut and assembled, the doll will move and dance,
circa 1905, by W.E. Mack, London. *Susan
Brown Nicholson collection*

Opposite Page Bottom Left Photo: Rare
silver Golliwogg rattle, 2 1/2 in. (6 cm),
English, circa 1910.

BRITISH MANUFACTURE.

The "Surprise" Packet Series 052

— OF —

WORKING TOY MODELS.

Charlie Chaplin.	Monkey up a Stick.
Harlequin.	Charley's Aunt.
The Policeman.	Gollywog.

Published by W. E. MACK, London, N.W.3.

Double page illustration from a Florence Upton Golliwogg book showing Golli off to prison, copyright 1901 by Longmans, Green & Co.

Ceramic plate, cup and saucer decorated with Golliwogg-style characters at play, no marks, circa 1910.

Ceramic plate, cup and saucer decorated with Golliwogg characters, no marks, circa 1910.

Page from *The Golliwogg's Christmas*, 1907, the most elusive volume in series. *Susan Brown Nicholson collection*

Sheet music *The Gollywog Two-Step* music by F. Brockett,1909. *Susan Brown Nicholson collection*

Golliwogg brass doorknocker, 6 in. with the same appearance as the Golli bank, English, circa 1910.

Bisque figure, 4 1/2 in. (12 cm), with unusual legs that swing by a pin joint, English, crown impressed, circa 1910.

Papier maché egg featuring scenes from Florence Upton's books, fleur-de-lis patterned interior and sticker attached giving permission for use by Longmans Green & Co., circa 1905. *Susan Brown Nicholson collection*

Fold-out Christmas greeting of Father Christmas with a suitcase on his back that opens to reveal an accordion fold-out of a day in the lives of a Teddy Bear and a Golliwogg, a superb example of an English novelty, circa 1907.

Two pages from Florence Upton's Golliwogg books cut down and framed; one shows building a boat and the other features Golli and wooden dolls in the water, circa 1906.

Christmas post card featuring Father Christmas with dolls and a Golliwogg, English, 1908, published by Raphael Tuck and Sons.

Two post cards featurig Golliwogg published by Raphael Tuck with art work by Agnes Richardson, English, circa 1910.

Post card "Stuffed Coon Series," Adolph Selig publisher, St. Louis, Mo., 1908. Post card "Birthday Greetings," B & P Co. Ltd., circa 1908. *Susan Brown Nicholson collection*

Golliwogg performers on a picture card published by Hugh Lang & Co., Liverpool. The players are identified as Spot, Master Bobbie Andrews, and Seth White, circa 1909. *Susan Brown Nicholson collection*

Post card with Christmas greetings and Golli with a velour face, circa 1907, English.

Figural Golliwogg booklet, 6 in. (15 cm), souvenir which opens to reveal accordian folded scenes of the seaside resort of Brighton, England, circa 1910, marked Valentine & Sons, Ltd., Dundee and London.

Greeting card with Golliwog strolling with Bonzo dog, also an English favorite, made in England, circa 1910. *Susan Brown Nicholson collection*

Two Christmas cards featuring Golliwogg with toys, teddy bears, and other animals. Left one marked "WEK, British Manufacture," blank inside for message, circa 1915. Right one is also English, circa 1910.

Three English post cards featuring Golliwogg; the bottom two as Christmas greetings, all designs taken from Florence Upton's books, circa 1903.

Ceramic tea set decorated with "The Golliwog's Joy Ride" illustration including a soapbox wagon pulled by a pig and other animals, English, circa 1915.

Child's feeding dish:, 7 1/2 in. (19 cm) diameter, featuring Golliwogg inside and outside, German, circa 1915.

Ceramic mug decorated with Golliwogg golfing, 3 in. (8 cm), English, circa 1915.

Post card with an illustration featuring a Golliwogg, signed Kennedy, published by C.W. Faulkner & Co. Ltd., series 1511, circa 1915. *Susan Brown Nicholson collection*

Cast metal bank, 6 in. (15 cm) with much of the paint remaining, English, circa 1915.

Dancing Golliwogg, 11 in. (28 cm), hand-made wooden dancing stick man jointed at the arms, hips, and knees, circa 1915.

Post card "The Cup that Cheers" by Phyllis Cooper of a child with Golliwogg, circa 1915. *Susan Brown Nicholson collection*

Post card "Tea Time" by H. & C. Marsh Lamiert, circa 1915. *Susan Brown Nicholson collection*

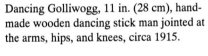

Golly! This is Fine

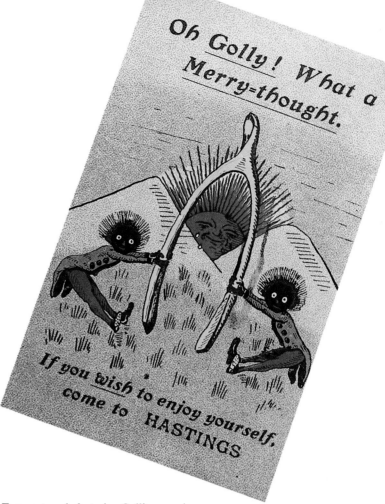

Two post cards featuring Golliwogg, circa 1915. *Susan Brown Nicholson collection*

Heavy ceramic feeding plate, 7 in. (18 cm), showing child, Teddy bear and Golliwogg, made in Czechoslavakia, circa 1920.

Baby's plate with decorations featuring Golliwogg with soapbox cart and waving a British flag, made by Wellesville China Co., circa 1920. Bill Boyd collection

Ceramic pitcher, 4 in. (10 cm), cup and saucer decorated with a scene featuring Golliwogg, English, circa 1920.

Dennis's "Dainty" Series Party Game "PINNIT" featuring Golliwogg. Wearing the enclosed blindfold, a player takes the head piece (included) with a straight pin inserted in the nose and tries to place the head onto the body. Points are scored where the pin is inserted, circa 1920.

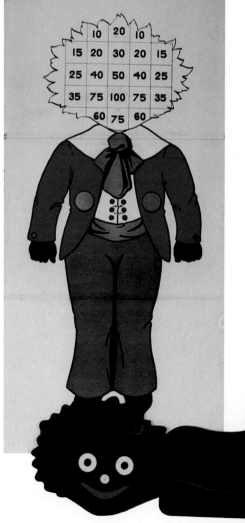

Cuebridge, a game played somewhat like pool, featuring Golliwogg and children on the free-standing bridge, no date, circa 1920.

Birthday card featuring Golliwogg and a velvet ribbon, Sharpes Classic made in England, circa 1920. The message inside reads, "Bertie Boy to my dear wife Nellie wishing her many Happy Returns on 23 year."

Page from a magazine drawn by Grace G. Drayton, the popular artist of the Dolly Dingle series, circa 1920. *Susan Brown nicholson collection*

Steiff stamp, 3 in. (8 cm). The Steiff Co. introduced a variety of stamps in the 1920s, among them this one featuring their version of Golliwogg.

Post cards featuring Golliwogg, circa
1920. *Susan Brown Nicholson collection*

Convalescent.

SWEET HONEYMOON

Mechanical Golliwogg, 6 in. made of
composition with painted features and
sealskin hair, non-removeable felt clothes,
key wound dancing toy, circa 1930.

Post cards showing Golli with children,
illustrations by Mabel Lucie Atwell. Susan
Brown Nicholson collection

Papier maché dish with Golliwogg
illustrated, 3 1/2 in. (9 cm), English, circa
1920.

Print showing Golliwogg and Bonzo the
dog, 12 in. (31 cm) square, circa 1930.

Advertisement for Le Golliwogg perfume in the earliest bottle design with sealskin hair used on the stopper. *Susan Brown Nicholson collection*

Advertising sign featuring Golliwogg, 17 in. (43 cm), heavy cardboard with a folding stand on back, printed in England, circa 1930.

Ceramic bank, 4 in. (10 cm), Golliwogg's head with googly eyes that move freely, English, circa 1935.

Perfume bottle and bottle stoppers made between 1920 and 1930 for a fragrance made in France by Vigny, Paris. The perfume was called "Le Golliwogg" and was presented in a satin-lined box; stoppers in several sizes were Golliwogg heads with sealskin hair.

Valentine made in Germany features Golliwogg, circa 1930. *Susan Brown Nicholson collection*

Decorated note paper on which Golliwogg is shown in colorful clothes, circa 1930. Susan Brown Nicholson collection

Tin toy clicker, 4 in. (10 cm), made in Germany, circa 1948. The clicker on the back causes the clown to hammer on Golly's head.

Golliwogg eau de cologne by Vigny, Paris, 6 in. (15 cm), in glass bottle with glass stopper made in the 1930s. Few of these bottles were made. Powder box, 5 in. (13 cm) of cardboard with satin overlay decorated with Golliwogg, circa 1930-1940, not marked, presumed to be European.

Tin sand pail, 3 1/2 in. (4 cm) featuring Golliwogg, made in England during the 1950s.

Hand-made stuffed Golliwogg on a plaster base, 12 in. shown playing a concertina and dressed to resemble a Robertson band member, circa 1950. *Bill Boyd collection*

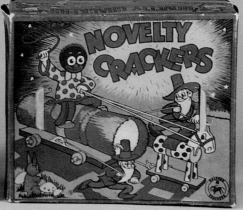

Fold-out valentine card dated 1942, made in Germany. *Bill Boyd collection*

English novelty party crackers, 5 1/2 in. (14 cm), boxed set of 12, circa 1950.

Uncut clothing sewing pattern in its original envelope, English, circa 1950s.

Jolly birthday card showing Golliwogg, teddy bear, and children in a story format published by Raphael Tuck & Sons Ltd., England, circa 1950.

Birthday cards featuring Golliwogg and teddy bear, British, circa 1950, marked "Printed in Great Britain, MIA cards."

Noddy's Ring Game made in conjunction with the Noddy series of books by J. W. Spear & Sons Ltd., Enfield, Middlesex, England, 1960.

Pelham puppet of Golliwogg, 10 in. (25 cm), stamped "Pelham, made in England" on the wooden crossbars.

Cardboard box featuring Golliwogg, 5 in. (13 cm), with squeaker, English, circa 1950, marked "Made in England/URAl"

Puzzle, 8 in. (20 cm), showing Golliwogg and Teddy bear, English, circa 1950.

Royal Doulton figurine "Golliwog," 5 1/2 in. (14 cm), Rd. no. 542482, © 1945, H N 2040, Doulton & Co. Ltd.

143

Royal Doulton Figurine, 7 in., of a Nanny
sitting with Golliwogg at her feet, © 1957.
Bill Boyd collection

Golliwogg as a Jack-in-the-box, 8 in. (20
cm) when opened, unmarked, circa 1960.

Cardboard picture, 2 1/2 in. (6 cm) X 6 in.
(15 cm) with Teddy bear and Golliwog on
both sides, English, circa 1950.

Book page, 10 in (25 cm) with illustration
"Teddy's Ride" by Travis Hart, shown
with Golliwogg, English, circa 1950.

Paper doll of Golliwogg designed by John Axe in a limited edition of 400, presented by the Toy Store to celebrate their 14th annual doll and teddy bear show in Toledo, Ohio, October, 1992.

Enameled metal jewelry charm with jointed limbs, 1 1/2 in. (4 cm), made in Scotland in the 1980s.

Marionette of Golliwogg, 12 in. (31 cm), with a painted wooden face, hands and feet and cotton clothes, made by Pelham, England, discontinued about 1992.

Three ceramic saucers hand-painted in oil paints with Golliwogg figures, circa 1965.

Cereal premium of Golliwogg, 2 in (5 cm), blue plastic figurine found in cereal boxes, stamped "Kelloggs" on bottom, circa 1980.

Robertson jig-saw puzzle and original envelope featuring Golliwogg, 5 in. (13 cm) X 6 1/2 in. (17 cm), circa 1940.

Santa paper decorations of Father Christmas with Golliwogg in his bag of toys, 3 in. (8 cm) each figure, English, 1980s.

James Robertson & Sons

The James Robertson Company, manufacturer of jams and preserves, first used the Golliwog as their logo around the turn of the century. It was in 1910 that Golly was first shown on labels, price lists and literature. The enameled brooch, still in vogue today, appeared initially in 1928 in the form of a golfer. Eleven years later it was discontinued because the metal was needed in the war effort. By 1946 Golly was back again and 10 years later premiums of all kinds were produced and eagerly collected. It was about this time that the eyes on the Golliwog's changed from looking straight ahead to looking to the left. This is a useful tool in determining the age of the products. By 1994 over 20 million Robertson Golliwog momentoes had been sent out to the joyful collectors.

Butler and Wilson rhinestone brooch of Golliwogg, 5 1/2 in. (14 cm), English, late 1980s and early 1990s.

146

Enameled metal pins of the Golliwogg image, 1 1/2 in. (4 cm), give-away premiums for the Robertson Jam Co. from 1930 to 1955. Robertson used Golliwogg sports players and musicians frequently in their advertising; also shown is a boy scout.

A single Golliwogg Robertson band figurine premium, 3 in. (8 cm) Plaster material with enameled color.

Enameled metal advertising display sign featuring Golliwogg, 14 in. (36 cm), for Robertson's Golden Shred Marmalade; sign made in England by Lodo Designs, (Mfrs.) Ltd., 8 Lonsdale Gardens, Royal Tunbridge, Wells, Kent, circa 1950.

Robertson Mince Meat tin, 3 1/2 in. (9 cm), the Golliwog logo was used on the label between 1930 and 1955.

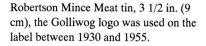

Enameled metal pins of the Golliwogg image that were Robertson Jam Co. premiums. The Golden Shred pin on the left is the earliest.

Ceramic figures of Golliwogg guitar players, 2 1/2 in (6 cm) used by the Robertson Jam Co. as a premium, circa 1950.

Enameled metal pin of the Golliwogg image, 1 1/2 in. (4 cm), given out as a premium; original style used from 1930 to 1955. "Golden Shred" is written on the vest.

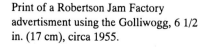

Bookmark with the Golliwogg image to advertise the Robertson Jam Company, 4 1/4 in. (11 cm), circa 1960.

Print of a Robertson Jam Factory advertisment using the Golliwogg, 6 1/2 in. (17 cm), circa 1955.

Post card with Golliwogg advertising
Robertson's Golden Shred Marmalade,
circa 1965.

Six of a series of pencil tops in the
Golliwogg image as sports and occupation
figures to advertise Robertson's Jam Co., 1
1/2 in. (4 cm), circa 1960-1965.

Pin-back, give-away premiums in four
colors with the Golliwogg image used by
Robertson Jam Co. in their advertising
after 1956.

Golliwogg as Robertson band member premiums, 2 1/4 in. (5.65 cm) made of enamel over plaster; several instruments with "Robertson" across front base, circa 1945.

Plate and cereal bowl premiums for Robertson Jam Co. with the Golliwogg image and the registered trademark of James Robertson and Sons Ltd., made in Staffordshire and produced after 1956.

Robertson's advertisements using the Golliwogg image, 9 in. (23 cm) X 12 in. (31 cm), these 1950s and 1960s store signs have folding stands on the backs.

Vinyl chair with tubular metal legs, 20 in. (51 cm), with Golliwogg's head as the back rest. This promotional item for Jas. Robertson & Sons amazingly retains its original box, circa 1960.

Ceramic bowl, 7 in. (18 cm) a premium for the jam company marked on back "Trade Mark of James Robertson Ltd.," circa 1960.

Creamware pitcher, 9 in. (23 cm), decorated with Golliwogg playing cricket, a Robertson's Jam Co. promotional made by The Silver Crane Co. circa 1960.

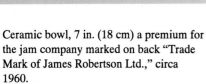

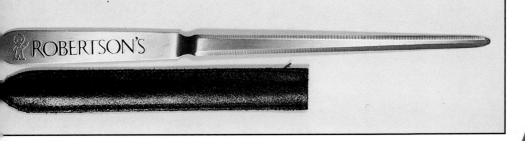

Letter opener, 9 1/2 in. (24 cm), of stainless steel with a sheath and marked with a Golliwogg and "Robertson's," the company for which it was a premium, circa 1960.

Advertising pencils that were premiums for Robertson's Gollicrush and Goldenshred and having the Golliwogg image as decoration, circa 1960.

Baseball cap in adult size of cotton with
appliqued vinyl Golliwogg as a promotion
for Robertson's products.

Knitted sweater patterns with the
Golliwogg image produced for
Robertson's products in several sizes,
1960s.

Canvas apron with Golliwogg advertising
Robertson's Viota products, circa 1970.

Cardboard coat hanger in the image of
Golliwogg, 9 1/2 in. (24 cm), that appears
to be a Robertson's premium.

Stainless steel and plastic cutlery in child's size with Golliwogg decoration.

Stickers, 2 in. (5 cm), showing Golliwog with band instruments used to promote Robertson's company; also found with a variety of sports equipment, circa 1970 to 1980.

Knitting sweater patterns with Robertson's version of Golliwogg, circa 1980. *Golliwog's Painting and Tracing Book*, English, circa 1965.

Playing cards in a box marked to celebrate the use of Golliwogg as the promotional image for Robertson's jams for fifty years.

Waxed paper bags with Golliwogg advertising Golden Shred and outlined to mount the Robertson's promotional music stickers, circa 1970 to 1980.

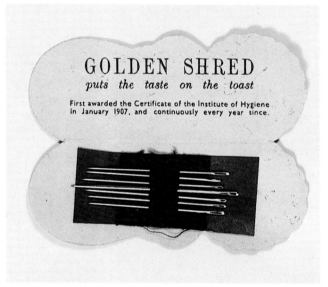

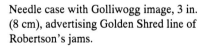

Needle case with Golliwogg image, 3 in. (8 cm), advertising Golden Shred line of Robertson's jams.

Plastic bank, 8 in. (20 cm), in the Golliwogg image with a money slot in the back of the head.

Plastic sheeting with Robertson's jam logo Golliwogg. Made as a picnic table cloth, circa 1985.

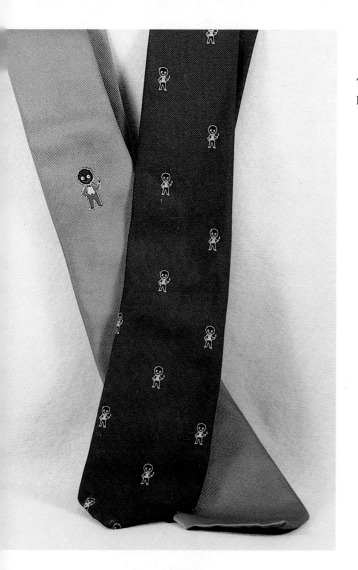

Two neckties with the Golliwogg image promoting Robertson's jams.

Backs of *I squeak* and Golliwogg doll.

Post card and greeting card with Golliwogg and friends advertising Robertson's Golden Shred Marmalade, l990s. *From the original in the Robert Opie collection*

Chapter Four
The Roosevelt Bears

Seymour Eaton and The Roosevelt Bears

The year was 1859. The place Epping, Ontario in Canada and the event was a birth that for ever more impacted the collecting community. Seymour Eaton came forth into a world far removed from the tumult of Canada's neighbor to the south. While a civil war raged in America, he grew up in a small provincial environment. Educated in Epping, he remained and chose what he imagined to be his life's work of teaching.

Eaton taught district school in the area for seven years, but a burning desire to write consumed him. Of course a writer needs to be paid for his efforts in order to survive, but the primary reason is not monetary or even the thrill of seeing one's name in print. The successful author has a mind brimming with ideas, a facility to turn ordinary words into beautiful phrasing and above all the knowledge that he has something of value to impart. As Seymour's life unfolded it became apparent that he possessed all of these attributes.

On January 15, 1884 he married Jennie Adair in Winnipeg, Manitoba and two years later the couple moved to Boston, Massachusetts where Eaton accepted a teaching post. During the six years of residency he saw several books published and was rewarded as an educator--becoming principal of Boston House College.

A relocation to Lansdowne, Pennsylvania, in the Philadelphia area, became home for the rest of his life and the base for all of his subsequent accomplishments. One year after teaching at the Drexel Institute of Technology, he became director of the business department and during this five year tenure he once again authored a number of books. Among his life's literary achievements he saw published *Dan Black Ed. and Propietor, Prince Domino And Muffles, Deuteronomy Jones-His Book*, several college textbooks, sermons on advertising and a drama "The Telepath". Seymour Eaton was a prolific writer for he also contributed daily to the *Chicago Record*, a four year position.

In 1900 he founded the Booklovers Library that ultimately evolved into a circulating library and book club. Two years later this enterprise claimed to be the largest of such establishments and an off-shoot seemed necessary. The resulting creation, The Tabard Inn, also saw Eaton as librarian.

The year 1903 became a milestone, for in that period he originated and edited the *Booklovers Magazine*. The first issue included a pastel portrait of the nation's president, Theodore Roosevelt, rendered by V. Floyd Campbell. Thus began the collaboration of Eaton with the artist. Seymour's first foray into fiction appeared in the magazine in 1904 with Campbell as illustrator and written under the pseudonym Paul Piper. Perhaps he felt that fiction was less esoteric and just an exercise in frivolity. A year later the *Booklovers Magazine* was sold and so began the body of work he became famous for.

During the first decade of the twentieth century the fourth estate found ample grist in the country's charismatic President. Newspapers abounded with the escapades of Teddy Roosevelt and principally with his role as the "Great White Hunter." The hunting expedition to Mississippi and the saga of the tied bear cub was cartooned by Clifford Berryman, the Teddy Bear was created by the Michtoms in America and Steiff in Germany and thus "bears" became the "hot" item.

Still using the pen name of Paul Piper, Eaton wrote a series of tales in verse form based on Roosevelt's hunting trip to Colorado, and starring two bears. They were illustrated by Campbell and the copyrights were filed in 1905 and 1906. The series ran in 20 newspapers for a period of 29 weeks and became so successful that the assumed name was abandoned in favor of Eaton's own. Unfortunately in 1906 a calamity occurred for Campbell fell victim to pneumonia, a deadly disease in those days, and did not recover.

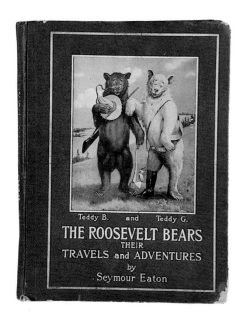

The Roosevelt Bears Their Travels and Adventures by Seymour Eaton, first in a series of four with illustrations by V. Floyd Campbell, ©1905 and 1906.

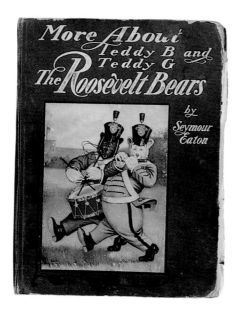

More About Teddy B and Teddy G The Roosevelt Bears by Seymour Eaton with illustrations by R. K. Culver, © 1906.

Teddy-B & Teddy-G The Bear Detectives by Seymour Eaton, © 1908 and 1909 by Edward Stern and Co., illustrated by Frances P. Wightman and William K. Sweeny. This is the most elusive of the first four volumes.

Teddy B and Teddy G The Roosevelt Bears Abroad, by Seymour Eaton, © 1908. This book is harder to find than the first two books.

The Traveling Bears is a rare version of Seymour Eaton's tales of Teddy B and Teddy G. published by Barse & Hopkins, N.Y., © 1909, profusely illustrated in black and white with 22 full page drawings, four in color. The cover and spine of this copy show damage but it is a significant edition.

T. R. In Cartoon by Raymond Gros, Saalfield Publishing Company, 1910, a collection of cartoons by various artists including 11 by Johnny Gruelle.

Theodore Roosevelt and the Teddy Bear

During the newspapers serial run, Seymour Eaton became the target of criticism. His detractors claimed that he was capitalizing on the popularity of Roosevelt and the Teddy Bear. One would hope, that like Liberace, he cried all the way to the bank. I think, however, that he was hurt and angered, for when the first eighteen episodes were published in book form by Edward Stern and Company, he chose to vindicate himself. In the introduction to *Teddy B and Teddy G The Roosevelt Bears Their Travels and Adventures* he wrote:

"This story has already stood the public test. It was published serially in 20 leading newspapers and has been received favorably by hundreds and thousands of children. No literary merit is claimed for it. The story is simply a good wholesome yarn arranged in a merry jingle and fitted to the love of incident and adventure which is evident in every healthy child. Since the name Roosevelt has been used in the title it may be of public interest to know that President Roosevelt and his boys have been pleased with the story as it appeared in serial form"

He was correct about the popularity for more episodes were demanded and ultimately created. For the second opus he selected R.K. Culver to illustrate. In *More About Teddy B and Teddy G The Roosevelt Bears*, Teddy B and G actually meet their namesake, the President, at the White House. The following volume, entitled *Teddy B. and Teddy G. The Roosevelt Bears Abroad* had Culver as illustrator, as well. By the time the fourth and final book, *Teddy B. and Teddy G. The Bear Detectives*, arrived in print, the drawings were rendered by Francis P. Wightman and William K. Sweeney. Edward Stern and Company remained as publisher and also held the license for the various products that followed.

Mr. Eaton extended his Teddy association by authoring *The Teddy Bears Musical Comedy*. During his lifetime he was a member of Poor Richards Club, on the staff of *Outlook* magazine, was associated with both *Vogue* magazine and *The New York Times* and founded the Shoppers Club. Death came on March 13, 1916 at the age of 58, having seen the popularity of his labor extended to all mediums. I'm sure he would be astounded to know that so many years later all that he composed is still loved by so many.

Teddy B. And Teddy G.'s Place In literature

The cover of the first bear book under Seymour Eaton's name, *Teddy B. and Teddy G. The Roosevelt Bears Their travels and Adventures*, show Teddy B and G in a pose that became the most frequently reproduced. They are standing on a hill wearing pince nez and carrying sombreros, a hatchet and a rifle. The large format is bound in dark green with the colored illustration by V. Floyd Campbell overlaid just above center.

More About Teddy B. And Teddy G. The Roosevelt Bears depicts the cover color artistry of R.K. Culver at the bottom of the charcoal bound volume and is off center. *The Roosevelt Bears Abroad*, illustrated by the same artist, has the inset color rendering above and to the right of midpoint against a blue gray background. The two artesans' works are so similar that unless especially noted, one would assume they were by the same person. The faces on Culver's bears may be somewhat fuller.

The first three tomes contained as many as 180 pages and sixteen full color illustrations. The last of the quartet, *The Bear Detectives*, with artwork by Francis P. Wightman and William K. Sweeney, was slimmer by about 30 pages and contained only half as many colored drawings. Since this is the most elusive of the four, it is probably safe to assume fewer copies were issued.

Theodore Roosevelt and the Teddy Bear booklet printed in honor of the President's 100th Birthday in 1958 when a festival was held in Giengen, Germany to celebrate the event and a 4-Teddy Campfire set was issued.

A lesser known edition, and one I have only seen one copy of, is simply entitled *The Traveling Bears*. Copyrighted in 1909 by Barse And Hopkins, it has many black and white designs and four full pages in color. Six years later the same publisher divided the four volumes into 10 separate books with fewer pages and artworks. They are extremely desirable even if one has the original four. The books are entitled *The Adventures of the Traveling Bears, The Traveling Detectives* and a series of eight with titles beginning *The Traveling Bears...* followed by *...in England, ...in Fairyland, ...at Play, ...in New York, ...in the East and West, ...in Outdoor Sports, ...Across the Sea* and *...Birthday*.

An average collector of Roosevelt Bear books may not be aware that Teddy B. and Teddy G. pop-up in unexpected places. One such arena is in the pocket size charmer published by Edward Stern in 1908, *The Snow Man's Christmas* which features Teddy G. on the inside cover, playing a role in the story, and being featured in eight colored pictures.

Cartoons by Johnny Gruelle from the Cleveland *Press* that appeared in *T. R. In Cartoon*.

Gruelle in the Cleveland Press.

TEDDY IN HOLLAND.

Gruelle in the Cleveland Press.

TEDDY IN PARIS.

The Traveling Bears series of ten books based on the four original Eaton books were published each with fewer pages and illustrations, © 1905 and 1906 by Seymour Eaton, © 1906 by E. Stern and Co., ©1915 by Barse and Hopkins.

Before publication in book format, the tales of Teddy B and Teddy G were serialized in several newspapers. The eigh[t] examples pictured appeared in the *Globe* in 1907 and eventually emerged as *The Roosevelt Bears Abroad*.

160

The Snow Man's Christmas, a small hardbound volume by Mary Herrick Bird illustrated in color by Joseph C. Claghorn was published by Edward Stern & Co. Inc. in 1908. It is interesting to note that starting on page 51, Teddy G enters the story; he also is shown on the inside cover and in eight illustrations.

A Cartoon History of Roosevelt's Career by Albert Shaw, published by The Review of Reviews, © 1910, includes many references to the bear hunting experience.

Roosevelt Laughing Bear, 25 in. (64 cm),
Columbia Mfg. Co., circa 1906. This short
gold mohair bear has glass eyes, felt pads,
open red painted wooden mouth with two
milk glass teeth. When his stomach is
pressed, the bear growls and opens his
mouth; his mouth also opens when his
head is turned. *The Roosevelt Bears Their
Travels and Adventures* by Seymour
Eaton, illustrated by V. Floyd Campbell in
1905 and 1906, Edward Stern & Co. Inc.
with black and white plus 16 full page
color illustrations.

A World of Roosevelt Bears

Edward Stern & Company, which first compiled the newspaper series and
ultimately printed them in four hard bound books, held the copyright for related
objects. This issue is somewhat clouded since various products neglect to state this
data. The possibility arises that the license was held for a short time and not picked
up when it ran out.

The popularity of Teddy B. and G. prompted the manufacturing of every
plaything imaginable, as well as useful products, for young and old alike. Post cards
in several series and stationary for more detailed missiles became available. The
local pubs had tip trays on the bar featuring their image while match safes and
jacknives, for the gentlemen, made an appearance.

The wonderful and colorful china manufactured by Buffalo Pottery is perhaps
the most highly coveted. The large milk jug is especially attractive, although smaller
pitchers were also made. Plates in a variety of sizes, as well as other accoutrements
necessary for table settings, can be counted. Milk glass, a popular item in the first
decade of the twentieth century, saw the bruins featured on candy containers and the
favorite hanging plates. Clear pressed or molded items such as paper weights or
butter molds and a set of nursery plates with the bruins in the center or around the
edge could be assembled.

A story and eventually china, featuring the "Rosa" bears are not actually
Eaton's offspring, but they certainly have a close resemblance and were inspired by
them. A succession of plates, some rather simple and others iridescent with pierced
rims, relate a continuing saga.

It was easy to by-pass copyright laws by making subtle changes or referring to
the bears by other names. A tin toy that rode a bicycle, weighted and string balanced,
came in a box labeled "Teddy Hustler." People today , accept it as a Roosevelt Bear
and add it to their collection. Unfinished copper findings, in figural formation, were
discovered in France a few years ago, brought back to America, fitted with clasps
and are now worn by the teddy aficionado.

A glorious array of teddy couture was fashioned ready-made or in pattern form
for the home sewer. Kahn and Mossbacher supplied a variety of clothes, including
sailor suits and sweaters, with Teddy B. or Teddy G. embroidered on the sleeve or
chest. According to a 1907 *Playthings* magazine, *The Ladies Home Journal* issued
a set of three outfit patterns for fifteen cents, that also featured the bears' names.
Even the Steiff Company, in Germany, produced teddies dressed in sweaters
bearing the Traveling Bears signature.

Beautifully lithographed fabrics in a size suitable for an impressive wall
hanging, but probably intended for a pillow covering, was introduced by Bernard
Ullman and Company. Several scenes from the tomes were utilized, but to find even
one is a thrill. Advertisers lured customers with their likeness while others were
certainly influenced by them. Everywhere one looked the Traveling Bears were
represented both in America and abroad.

Were Eaton's detractors correct in decrying he was riding on the teddy bear's
coat tails? In a sense, yes. Everyone gets an idea from someplace, whether
consciously or subconsionsly, and Seymour Eaton had a good one. So good in fact,
that I'm sure the nay sayers fervently wished it had been theirs. Teddy B. and G. rose
in popularity every year and stayed in good esteem all of the author's life. Certainly
he lived to see his anger tempered by the enormous response to what he had created.

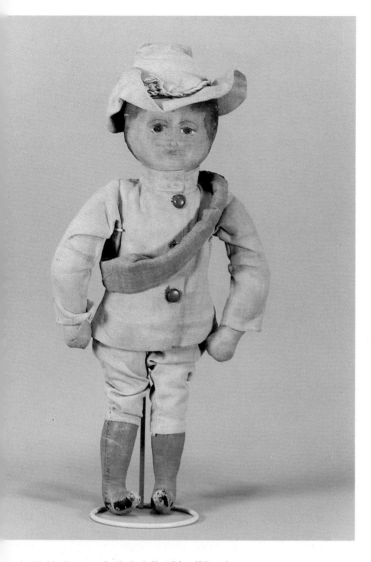

Teddy Roosevelt cloth doll, 15 in. (38 cm), made of cloth and dressed as a Rough Rider with painted features and hair, and boots painted to simulate leather, circa 1900, American.

Clifford Berryman Bear, 13 in. (33 cm), brown and white mohair with felt airbrushed paws fashioned by Steiff in conjunction with Linda Mullins, 1986.

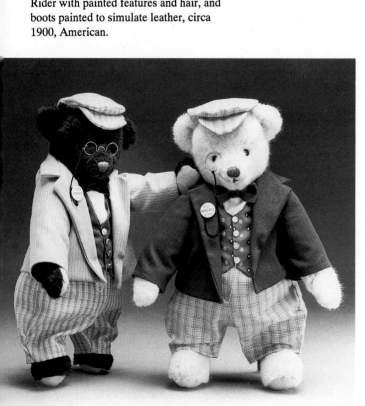

Teddy B and G Teddy Bears, 17 in. In the early 1980s, the first plush representation of the Roosevelt Bears became a reality. The charming, fully clothed, bruins were the brainstorm of Dottie Ayers and Donna Harrison of the Calico Teddy, a shop in Baltimore, Md. They were produced by Dean's Childplay Toys Ltd. of Great Britain, and proved an instant success. *Courtesy of Dottie Ayers*

THOSE MISCHIEVOUS BEARS FROM THE ROOSEVELT ERA
ARE NOW AVAILABLE IN SIGNED,
LIMITED EDITION OF 1,000 PIECES EACH.

Teddy B & Teddy G were designed and are being distributed exclusively by: D & D PRODUCTIONS, INC.

The Bears were handcrafted in England by Dean's Childplay Toys, Ltd.

These 17″ fully-jointed plush bears are authentically dressed in the early 1900's style*. Because of their unique body design, we are offering these lovely bears 'bare'. *Clothing fabric may vary slightly.

For prices and other information please write:
D & D Productions, Inc.
22 East 24th Street, Baltimore, MD 21218   (301) 366-7011
Dealer inquiries welcome, please enclose business card.

Roosevelt Bear, 4 in. (10 cm), in Rough
Rider costume by Canadian artist Trudy
Yelland, 1991.

Teddy Roosevelt Bear, 14 in. (36 cm),
made by the Toy Works in a limited
edition of 1000 for the Adirondack
Chamber of Commerce, numbered, 1993.

Roosevelt Bears, 2 in. (5cm), made of a
clay composition with jointed limbs,
designed by April Whitcomb and distributed by Schmid in 1992. Several designs
came in a presentation box shaped and
outfitted as a steamer trunk.

Teddy B and Teddy G Roly-Polys, 1 1/2 in., finely detailed and made in 1993 by Canadian bear artist Trudy Yelland.

The First Series:

No. 14. The Roosevelt Bears on the Iceberg

No. 16. The Roosevelt Bears at the Circus

No. 10. The Roosevelt Bears at Niagara Falls

No. 12. The Roosevelt Bears Take an Auto Ride

No. 4. The Roosevelt Bears on a Farm

The Second Series:

No. 26. The Roosevelt Bears at Independence Hall

No. 18. They put crackers along the wire

No. 32. The Roosevelt Bears at Washing-
ton

No. 31. The Roosevelt Bears as Hunters

The Third Series:

No. 29. The Roosevelt Bears Go Fishing

No. 27. The Roosevelt Bears Celebrate the
Fourth

No. 19 "From noon til night..."

Roosevelt Bear post cards were issued in 1906 and 1907 by E. Stern & Co. Inc. in four groups:

The first sixteen are from *Teddy B and Teddy G- Their Travels and Adventures*, illustrated by V. Floyd Campbell.

The second series numbered 17-32 are the work of R. K. Culver who illustrated *More About Teddy B and Teddy G*. These 32 cards have titles.

The third series, also numbered 17-20, have quotes from the books and are harder to locate.

A fourth group, consisting of at least five cards and possibly more are from *The Roosevelt Bears Abroad*, also illustrated by Culver, and are not numbered. *Susan Brown Nicholson collection*

No. 20 "At the Liberty Bell..."

The Fourth Series:

The Roosevelt Bears in Ireland

The Roosevelt Bears in Scotland

The Roosevelt Bears in England

The Roosevelt Bears Return from Abroad

Roosevelt Bear postcard of unusual design and rare to find with overalls that are sanded for striking matches, 1907. *Susan Koenker Collection*

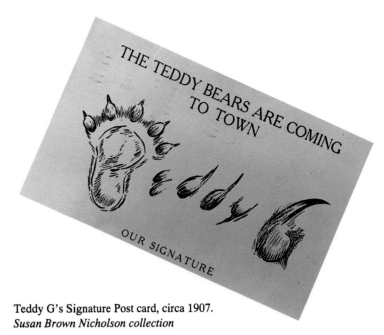

Teddy G's Signature Post card, circa 1907. *Susan Brown Nicholson collection*

Teddy B embossed postcard, circa 1907.

Roosevelt Bear campaign post card showing the bear wearing spectacles, carrying a Rough Rider hat and a flag, circa 1907.

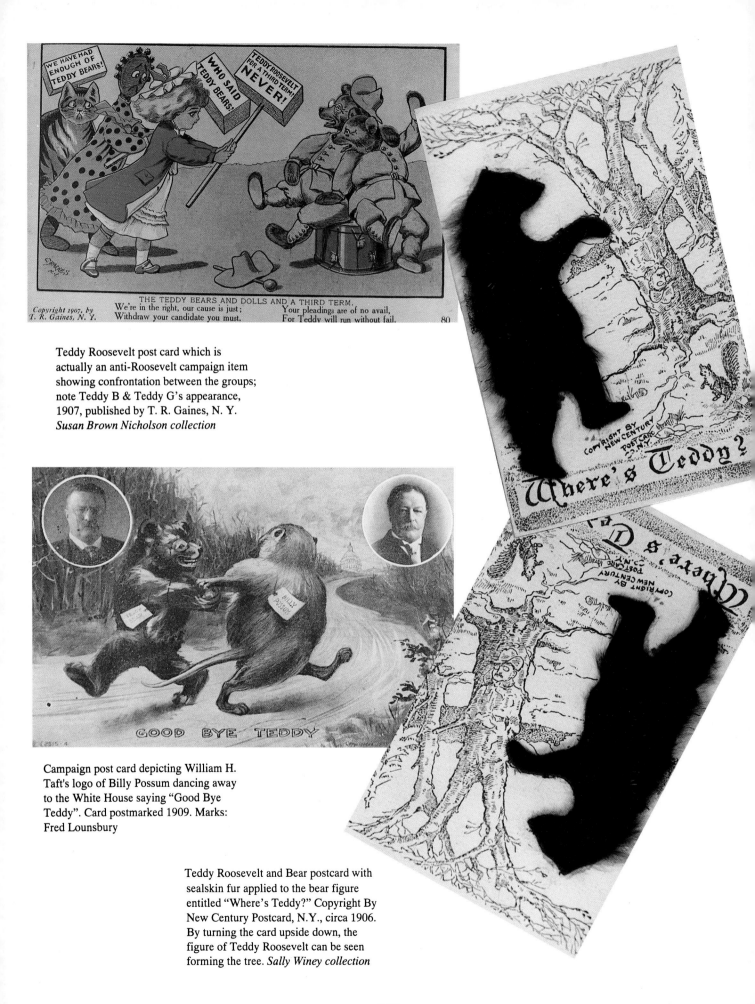

Teddy Roosevelt post card which is
actually an anti-Roosevelt campaign item
showing confrontation between the groups;
note Teddy B & Teddy G's appearance,
1907, published by T. R. Gaines, N. Y.
Susan Brown Nicholson collection

Campaign post card depicting William H.
Taft's logo of Billy Possum dancing away
to the White House saying "Good Bye
Teddy". Card postmarked 1909. Marks:
Fred Lounsbury

Teddy Roosevelt and Bear postcard with
sealskin fur applied to the bear figure
entitled "Where's Teddy?" Copyright By
New Century Postcard, N.Y., circa 1906.
By turning the card upside down, the
figure of Teddy Roosevelt can be seen
forming the tree. *Sally Winey collection*

Trade card for jewelry rings depicting
Roosevelt Bear in a chair smoking a cigar
blowing the advertised smoke rings.
Hayden W. Wheeler and Co., New York,
circa 1907.

Trade card depicting Teddy B. and Teddy
G. to advertise the A. Lezius Tea Co., circa
1907. *Susan Brown Nicholson collection*

Trade cards somewhat smaller than post
cards depicting the Roosevelt bears
advertising Estey organs of Brattleboro,
Vermont, circa 1909.

Advertising booklet depicting the Roosevelt bears at baking school, given out by the Fleischmann Company, makers of yeast, © 1906-1907 by Seymour Eaton and Edward Stern & Co.

Writing tablet depicting the Roosevelt bears, 6 1/2 in. (17 cm) X 9 1/2 in. (24 cm), distributed by G. Sommers, 1907. 100 ruled pages with 10 different designs. *Susan Brown Nicholson collection*

Bread advertising premium and needle packet shaped as Teddy Bear, circa 1910.

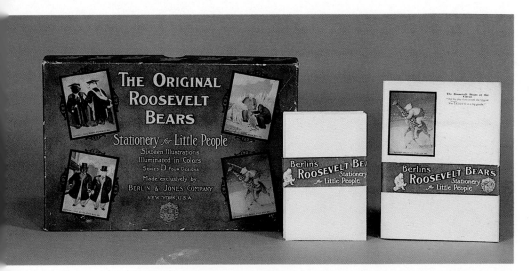

The Original Roosevelt Bears Stationary for Little People with four designs and envelopes, made by Berlin & Jones Company, New York, ©1906 by Edw. Stern & Co. Inc.

Black and white illustration removed from one of Eaton's books and hand colored and framed.

Lithograph, 20 1/2 in. (52 cm) X 21 in. (53 cm), of the two Roosevelt bears as found on the cover of the first volume by Seymour Eaton, *The Roosevelt Bears their Travels and Adventures*, circa 1907, rare.

Ceramic dinner and dessert plates decorated with printed scenes from the stories and text, made by Buffalo pottery, © Edw. Stern & Co, 1906.

Lithograph print on linen cloth, 24 in., of the Roosevelt bears, produced by Bernard Ulmann & Company, 1907. *Susan Koenker Collection*

Ceramic mug, 3 1/4 in. (8 cm), decorated with a scene from the cover of Seymour Eaton's first book about the Roosevelt bears, produced for Edw. Stern & Co. by Buffalo Pottery, 1906.

Ceramic milk pitcher made by Buffalo Pottery with elaborate colored transfer printed decoration featuring the Roosevelt bears scenes from the stories and portions of the text, © Edw. Stern and Co., 1906.

Ceramic cup and saucer decorated with Teddy B on one side and Teddy G on the other, made by Carlsbad China in Austria, circa 1908.

Ivory china feeding dish, 9 in. (23 cm), with gold and roses trim, a poem and a scene from the first Seymore Eaton book in the center, and two more scenes around the edge."They slid down ropes and hit the ground and landed in Chicago safe and sound." This unusual shape slopes up and then down to form a well, 1906. Marked: Royal lady plate/ patented/ U.S. Feb.7, 1906/ Germany, Great Britain, France, Canada.

Milk glass alphabet plate, 7 in. (18 cm), with the Roosevelt bears as on the cover of Seymour Eaton's first book, circa 1907.

Milk glass mustard jar, 3 1/2 in. (9 cm), decorated with the Roosevelt bears in relief in a mountain setting. Originally, this had more color, the remains of green and gold is evident, circa 1908.

Milk glass candy container, 3 3/4 in. (10 cm), in the shape of a suitcase with a metal handle and bottom slide-out tray, gold trim, and decorated with an illustration of the Roosevelt bears as they appeared on the cover of the first Seymour Eaton book. Marked on the side, "pat. apl'd. for", circa 1907.

Ceramic plate, 5 1/4 in. (13.65 cm), one of a series called "The Bear Hunt," circa 1910. The verse reads, "When Rosa Cried He Has Been Here! / Then Teddy blanched and said/ We'd better not go near his trail/ or we'll be with the Dead".

Ceramic plate "Digging the Ditch at Panama," 7 in. (18 cm), part of a series with Roosevelt bears illustrated and a pierced rim with some irredescence added. The verse reads, "To finish this great work/ We need no foreign aid,/ For we can do it all ourselves/ With spirit and with spade," circa 1910.

Intaglio glass paperweight, 3 in. (8 cm) square, molded with the Roosevelt Bears as they appeared on the cover of Seymour

Ceramic plate, 8 in., with a pierced rim, part of a series, entitled "Teddy and Rosa in the G.O.P." The verse reads, "The Grand Old Party's sale/ with Roosevelts Guiding hand/ And peace and plenty will prevail/ Throughout our native land," circa 1910.

Oval glass bread plate "A Square Deal,"
with frosted portrait of Theodore
Roosevelt in the center and bears around
the edge; a campaign item, circa 1908.

Cardboard puzzle, 15 in. (38 cm) x 9 in. (23 cm), with bears in the manner of The Roosevelt Bears; circa 1920.

Three pressed glass nursery plates, 6 1/4 in. (16 cm), from a series with the Roosevelt bears around the rim and rhymes in the center: left, Bo Peep; center, bears in a pose like Seymour Eaton's first book cover; and right, "This little pig went to market," probably American, circa 1909.

Blue cotton overalls embroidered Teddy B
on the bib, possibly made by Kahn and
Mossbacher, shown on a 9-inch bear and
available to fit several sizes, circa 1907.

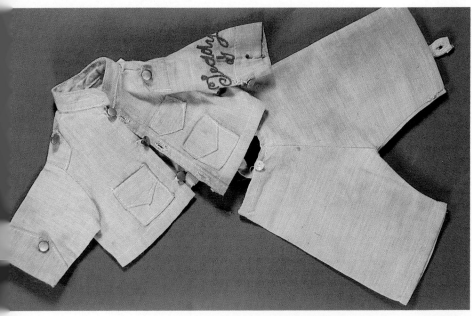

Rough Rider ensemble with Teddy G embroidered in red on the sleeve, possibly made by Kahn and Mossbacher in a size to fit a 10-inch (25 cm) teddy bear, circa 1910.

Tin tip tray, 4 3/4 in. (12 cm), with crimped corners and a scene of the Roosevelt bears as they appeared on the cover of the first Seymour Eaton book. This advertised The Oxford Bank of Newcomerstown, Ohio, © 1906 by Edward Stern and Co. Inc. The poem at top reads, "Two Roosevelt Bears had a home out west/ In a big ravine near a mountain crest." The brown edges illustrate black bears in a variety of poses.

Plated silver match safe, 2 3/4 in. (7 cm), with Teddy B carrying a stick and wearing a Rough Rider hat. The reverse side shows three Teddies dancing, circa 1906, no mark.

Copper molded brooch, 1 in. (3 cm), replicating the Roosevelt bears, found unfinished in France, circa 1910.

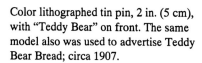

Color lithographed tin pin, 2 in. (5 cm), with "Teddy Bear" on front. The same model also was used to advertise Teddy Bear Bread; circa 1907.

California delegate's badge for the election of Theodore Roosevelt for President at the California Progressive Convention of 1912, 4 1/2 in. (5 cm), brass.

Cast iron mechanical bank "Teddy and the Bear" made by the J. E. Stevens Co. in 1907.

Sterling silver spoon with two bears climbing a tree after stealing Teddy Roosevelt's hat, circa 1907.

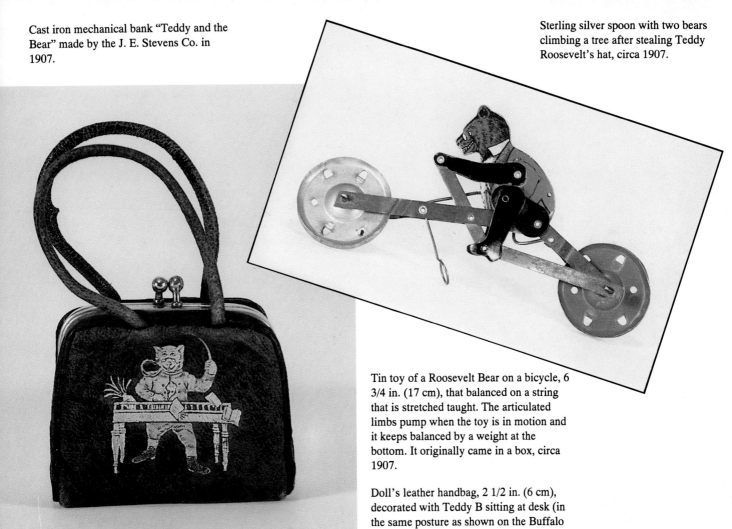

Tin toy of a Roosevelt Bear on a bicycle, 6 3/4 in. (17 cm), that balanced on a string that is stretched taught. The articulated limbs pump when the toy is in motion and it keeps balanced by a weight at the bottom. It originally came in a box, circa 1907.

Doll's leather handbag, 2 1/2 in. (6 cm), decorated with Teddy B sitting at desk (in the same posture as shown on the Buffalo china milk jug), circa 1906.

Silver figural bear jacknife, 2 3/4 in. (7 cm), with Teddy B on one side and Teddy G on the reverse, made in Germany, circa 1907.

Teddy B and Teddy G Walk off, bidding
all a fond farewell.

Bibliography

Books

Cieslik, Jurgen and Marianne, Knopf Im Ohr, Marianne Cieslik Verlag, 1989.

Commire, Ann, ed., *Something About the Author*, Gale research Co., Detroit, Mich., 1984.

Falk, Byron A., Jr., and Valerie R. Falk, ed., *Personal Name Index*, Roxbury Data Interface, Succasunna, N. J.

Fisher, Margery, ed., *Who's Who in Childrens Books*, Holt, Rinehart and Winston, 1975.

Garrison, Susan, *The Raggedy Ann and Raggedy Andy Family Album*, Schiffer Publishing Ltd., West Chester, Pa., 1989.

Girouard, Mark, Life in the English Country House, Yale University Press, New Haven, Conn., 1978.

Lenard, Alexander, *Winnie Ille Pu*, E.P. Dutton, N.Y., 1960.

Lyttleton, Edith, *Florence Upton, Painter*, Longman's, Green and Co., Ltd., New York, Toronto, Bombay, Calcutta and Madrid, 1926.

Marquis, Albert Nelson, ed., *Who's Who in America*, The A. N. Marquis Company, Chicago, 1943.

Milne, Christopher, *The Enchanted Places*, Eyre Methuen Ltd., Great Britain, 1974.

Mullins, Linda, *Teddy Bears Past and Present*, Hobby House Press. Cumberland, Md., 1986.

Nicholson, Susan Brown, *Teddy Bears On Paper*, Taylor Publishing Co. 1985.

Oxford Companion to Children's Literature, Oxford University Press, 1984.

Quayle, Eric, ed., *Collector's Book of Children's Books, The,*Clarkson N. Potter, 1971.

Sokolski, Mia, *The Romance of the Captain and Winnie the Bear*, (Self-published), Canada, 1992

Swann , Thomas Burnett, *A.A. Milne*, Florida Atlantic University. Twayne Publishers. N.Y. 1971.

Thwaite, Ann. *A.A. Milne, The Man Behind Winnie-the-Pooh*, Random House, 1990.

————, *The Brilliant Career of Winnie-the-Pooh*, Methuen, Great Britian, 1992.

Periodicals

Cleff, Susan, "Meet the Golliwog," *The Antique Trader*, Dubuque, Iowa, July 1992.

Lauver, Barbara, "America's Own Raggedy Ann and Raggedy Andy,"
Collector's Showcase, June, 1989.

Moose, Charles R. "The Naming of the Teddy Bear," *Teddy Bear and Friends*, June 1990.

Nicholson, Susan Brown, The Golliwogg Collectibles," *Spinning Wheel*, Jan./ Feb. 1981.

Schoonmaker, Patrica, "The 80th Anniversary of The Roosevelt Bears," *Teddy Bear and Friends*, June 1986.

Price Guide

While every effort is made to be accurate the prices listed are meant to be a *guide* to aid the collector and are not to be taken as absolute. Neither the author or the publisher assumes any responsibility to the collector when either buying or selling.

Winnie The Pooh

1st edition Books-$200-$500 depending on condition and dust jackets

1st edition Song Books-$85-$150 depending on condition and dust jackets.

Later edition books-$10+

Page	Item	Price
19	Fabric	$75-$100
20	Pop-up Book	$165-$195
	Winnie The Pooh Book, Perks Pub.	$25-$35
21	Golden Book	$5-$10
	Enchanted Places	$20-$30
	Pooh Cook Book	$35-$45
22	Magazine Page	$15-$25
	The Path Through The Trees	$20-$30
	Poohs Pot 0 Honey	$20-$25
	Pu der Bar	$50-$60
	Childrens Digest	$20-$25
23	Paper doll	$10-$15
	B P Gas station Books	$20-$25
25	Agnes Brush Pooh	$250-$350
	Agnes Brush Kanga/Roo	$250-$350
26	Agnes Brush Piglet	$250-$350
27	Agnes Brush Owl, Rabbit, Tigger and Eeyore	$250-350 each
	Knickerbocher Kanga/Roo	$75-$80
28	Gund Pooh	$100-$150
	Knickerbocker Piglet	$75-$80
	Gund velvet Poohs	$40-$50
29	Gund Tigger, Eeyore, Kanga/Roo and Piglet	$40-$50 each
	R. John Wright Christopher Robin I	$1,800-$2,000 M.I.B.
30	R. John Wright Christopher Robin II	$1,700-$1,800 M.I.B.
	R. John Wright Tigger, Kanga, Roo, Eeyore, Piglet and Pooh	$450-$550 each. $2,500 for set.
	R. John Wright 18 in Pooh	$950-$1,500
31	R. John Wright Piglets 7 in and 9 in	$325-$395
	R. John Wright Pooh in chair	$950-$1,050
	R. John Wright Pocket Piglet	$225 issue price 1994
32	R. John Pocket Pooh	$325+, and rising
	Wilkinson Poohs	$45-$70
33&		
34	Gabrielle Animals & Pooh	$75-$95
34	Eeyore Backpack	$20-$30
35	Piglet 1990s	$25-$30
	Piglet 1980s	$60-$70
	Pooh hot water bottle	$75-$85
	Grad Nite Pooh	$75-$85
36	Sears Pooh	$50-$100
	Pooh stocking	$45-$50
	Carol Stewart Pooh	$275-$350
	Sherri Dodson Pooh	$85-$125
37	Pooh bowls	$275-$375
	Pooh pitcher	$175-$200
38	Pooh oval bowl	$375-$425
	Pooh pitcher	$175-$200
	Pooh tray	$300-$325
38&		
39	Pooh Gift set	$195-$225
39	Paper dolls	$20-$25 repro., orig. $75-$125
40&		
41	Puzzles page	$85-$95
41	Game	$125-$145
42	Framed game pictures	$15-$20 each
43	Records	$20-$25
44	Needlepoint	$165-$175
	Prints	$55-$60 set
44,45, 46,47	Art Gallery	$200-$275
47	Piglet	$750+ for set
	Figurine	$100-$120
	Heffalump	$35-$45
48	Stamps	$15-$25 each
	Button	$10-$15
	Head Pin	$90-$95
49	Buttons	$8-$10
	Dress	$10-$20
	Silver pendant with charms	$295-$325
50	Cut-outs	$20-$30
	Enamel boxes	$110-$195
	Print	$35-$40
	Watch	$75-$125
51	Telephone	$100-$150
	Willitts Mug	$20-$30
	Selandia Mug	$5-$10
	Switch plate	$25-$35
52	Hankie	$15-$20
	Tumbler	$5-$10
	Keyring	$10-$15
	Ornament	$20-$30
53	Backpack	$20-$30
	Watch	$55-$65
	Tray	$25-$35
	Animation cel	$800-$1,000
54	Ornament	$20-$30
	Mug	$35-$40
	Jumping Jack	$35-$40
55	Cards, writing paper	$8-$10

Raggedy Ann

1st edition Books $75-$195 depending on condition, dust jackets and or/boxes.
Later editions-$25-$55
By other authors or illustrators-$25-$45

57	Sheet music	$35
	Quacky and Danny	$550 each
58	Ann store display	$1400
59	Sheet music	$35
	Ann Awake/Asleep	$400
60	Puzzles	$100
	Ann	$225
	Ann, 2-tone hair	$195
61	Arthur	$75
	Watering can	$30
	Shoe shining kit	$30
62	Poster	$50+
63	Volland Ann/Andy	$1,300-$1,600 each
	Little Brown Bear	$250
64	Clock	$35
65	Volland Beloved Belindy	$3,000-$4,500
66&		
67	Little Eva's	$1,200-$1,800 pair, depending on condition, original clothing etc.
68	Exposition Doll	$4,500+
68&		
69	Mollyes Ann/Andy	$900-$1,800
69	Buddy	$225-$245
70	Georgene Andy	$450-$550
	Beloved Belindy	$1,500-$1,800
71	Ann-replaced clothes	$225-$245
	32 in Ann and Andy	$650-$750 each
	19 in Ann and Andy	$450-$550
	Ann and Andy awake/asleep	$350-$400 each
72&		
73	Awake/asleep Ann/Andy	$350-$550
73	Ironing Ann	$425-$475
	Georgene Ann-horse print dress	$300-$350
	Camel	$800-$1,000
74	Knickerbocker Beloved Belindy	$650-$750
	Knickerbocker Beloved Belindy	M.I.B. $1,500
	Handmade Beloved Belindy	$450-$550
75	Knickerbocker Ann/Andy	$M.I.B. $65-$85 each
	Talking Ann	$150-$200
76	Ann and Andy	M.I.B. $165-$185
	Knickerbocker Ann & Andy miniatures	$20-$30 each
	Pillow	$5-$7
77	Puppets pg 77.	$10-$12 each
	Musical Andy	$150-$175
78	Camel	$150, M.I.B. $325
	30 in pair Raggedy's	$65-$75 each
78,79, 80	Hand made Raggedy's	$45-$75 each
80	Hasbro	$34-$40

	Carol Furgeson Anns	$45-$50 each
81	Valentine	$95-$100
	Paper dolls	$175-$225
82	Blocks	$100-$125
82&		
83	Paper dolls	$12-$15 each
83&		
85	Railroad puzzle	$175-$195
84	Bowls	$60-$90 each
85	Game	$45-$55
	Tea set	$145-$155
86	Marionette	$70-$80
	Iron	$8-$10
	Records	$5-$8
86&		
87	Ornaments, indiv.,	$12-$20; set of 6, $125-$130
87	Pattern	$20-$30
	Pendant	$50-$55
88	Ideal dolls	$350-$375 pair
	Ornament	$6-$8
	Charms	$75-$125 each
	Paper doll book	$10-$12
89	Windsock	$15-$20
	Niagara plate	$45-$50
	12 in Ann & Andy	$35

Golliwoggs

1st edition books $250-$500. Perhaps more for Christmas issue.

91	Joan Allen platter	$675-$695
96	*Vege-Men's Revenge*	$250-$300
	The Teddy Bearoplane Playtime/Saucy Squirrel	$250-$275
		$35-$65
97	Books	$35-$65
98	*Teddy Bear Book*	$85-$95
	Teddys Tea Party	$45-$55
	Magic Island	$75-$80
99	*Maxie/Gollybear*	$35-$45
	Golly Runs Away	$55-$65
	Toy Town Day by Day sold with artists original cover rendition	$950
	Georgie Golliwog sold with artists original cover rendition	$1,250.
100	*Golly I Squeak*	$95-$100
	Teddy, Golly & Bunny	$80-$90
	Noddy Book	$45-$50
	Noddy Tin	$75-$85
101	*Rufty Tufty Makes A House*	$55-$60
102	Book	$15-$20
103	Early dolls	$1,750-$1,850 pair
104	2 in doll	$95-$100
	10 in pair	$275-$325 each
104-117	Hand made dolls	$70-$300 depending

Index

About the Author

Dee Hockenberry is the author of five previous books, all dealing with collectibles and soft toys. She is a contributing editor to three Teddy Bear magazines, two in the United States and one in England. Well known in the field of Steiff products, she often lectures on the subject and operates a mail order business of vintage toys. She and her partner in this enterprise may be seen at select shows including the twice-a-year "Atlantique" City extravaganza. Dee started in the business as a Teddy Bear designer and continues to supply shops with her creations both in the United States and abroad. Her husband, Tom, photographs all her works. They are the parents of two grown children.